SAMUEL TAYLOR COLERIDGE

Selected
Poems

SAMUEL TAYLOR COLERIDGE

Selected Poems

GRAMERCY BOOKS
New York • Avenel

Introduction and compilation
Copyright © 1996 by Random House Value Publishing, Inc.

This 1996 edition is published by Gramercy Books,
distributed by Random House Value Publishing, Inc.,
40 Engelhard Avenue,
Avenel, New Jersey 07001.

Random House
New York • Toronto • London • Sydney • Auckland

Printed and bound in the United States

Library of Congress Cataloging-in-Publication Data

Coleridge, Samuel Taylor 1772–1834
[Poems. Selections]
Samuel Taylor Coleridge, Selected poems / Samuel Taylor Coleridge.
p.   cm.
ISBN: 0–517–15028–X
I. Title.
PR4478.A1   1996
821'.7—dc20   95–49110   CIP

8 7 6 5 4 3 2 1

CONTENTS

The Rime of the Ancient Mariner

Christabel

INTRODUCTION

By all contemporary accounts Samuel Taylor Coleridge was considered one of the most brilliant men of the English Romantic movement. John Stuart Mill stated that he was "the most systematic thinker of our time" and one of "the two great seminal minds of England." William Hazlitt, a contemporary and friend, wrote that Coleridge was "the only person I ever knew who answered to the idea of a man of genius." And today, he remains one of the most popular poets in English literature. However, the conclusion of many of Coleridge's own friends and scholars and critics since has been that he never fulfilled the promise of his talents.

Samuel Taylor Coleridge was born on October 21, 1772. He was the youngest of ten children of the Reverend John Coleridge, the vicar of Ottery St. Mary in Devon. Coleridge was a precocious and intelligent child and at an early age he became captivated by the fantastic tales from the Arabian Nights; his taste for the strange and wonderful would later influence his supernatural poems like "Christabel." When Coleridge was nine his father died and he was sent to school at Christ's Hospital, London. Charles Lamb, a schoolmate, wrote that Coleridge was "a poor friendless boy" and "alone among six hundred playmates." Losing the security of home was a traumatic experience for Coleridge—for the rest of his life he was haunted by nightmares about his harsh life at the school. Despite this he was an excellent student whom Lamb called a "Logician, Metaphysician, Bard!" When Coleridge went up to Jesus College, Cambridge, in October 1791 at the age of nineteen, he was one of the best-read students. However, his stay at Cambridge was turbulent.

Depressed after a failed romance with one Mary Evans and falling deeply into debt, Coleridge ran away and joined the Light Dragoons on December 4, 1793, under the name of Silas Tomkyn Comberbacke. His military career was short, however, as his brothers tracked him down and bought him out of the service, returning him to Cambridge. On a visit to Oxford in June 1794, Coleridge met Robert Southey and together they planned to start a Utopian society in America. Twelve young men with twelve wives would form a "pantisocracy"—Coleridge invented the name— as an "experiment in human perfectibility." Since the plan dictated that Coleridge have a wife, out of expediency he became engaged to Sarah Fricker, Southey's future sister-in-law. The scheme soon collapsed when funding for the venture failed to materialize—Southey's aunt refused to give them the money. However, Coleridge went through with the wedding and married Sarah in October 1795, and then left Cambridge without his degree.

The marriage was at first successful and the couple moved to a cottage in Nether Stowey. He endeavored to make a living from his poetry, journalism, and lecturing. Supporting a family for him would be one of his major preoccupations and the source of financial stress for the rest of his life, as he wrote: "The two giants leagued together, whose most imperious commands I must obey, however reluctant—their names are BREAD and CHEESE." The couple had two sons, Hartley and Berkeley, and a daughter, Sara.

On June 5, 1797, Coleridge visited William Wordsworth and his sister Dorothy at Racedown in Dorset, beginning one of the greatest literary friendships and collaborations in literary history. Coleridge and Wordsworth inspired each other to new heights of achievement. In 1798 they jointly published *Lyrical Ballads*, considered one of the most revolutionary volumes in English verse. During their years of close friendship, Coleridge wrote his greatest poetry, including "The Rime of the Ancient Mariner," "Kubla Khan," and "Frost at Midnight."

However, this creative period for Coleridge would be short-lived. His chronic rheumatism and general ill-health began to plague him. Even worse, by 1802, he had become addicted to his medication, laudenum—opium dissolved in alcohol—which began to drain his creative energies. Soon his troubled marriage was further weakened when he fell in love with Sara Hutchinson, Wordsworth's sister-in-law—one of the factors that led to a permanent separation from his wife. The emotional turmoil and financial stress of his drug addiction would eventually become so severe that by 1816 Coleridge put himself under the care of Dr. James Gillman, living the last eighteen years of his life in Gillman's Highgate, London home. There he regained some control over his addiction and found some peace of mind. He spent his last years lecturing and writing on literature and philosophy. Near the end of his life he became the center of a small circle of admirers with whom, from 1822 on, Coleridge held a "Thursday-evening class." He died in Highgate, London, on July 25, 1834.

Coleridge's reputation after his death became that of a man of who failed to fulfill his early promise, as echoed by Thomas Carlyle: "To the man himself Nature had given, in high measure, the seed of a noble endowment; and to unfold it had been forbidden him." But judging a person by what he was unable to accomplish is clearly unfair. As the poems included in the volume clearly attest, Coleridge remains one of the most popular and influential poets in English literature. And we must agree wholeheartedly with Coleridge when he wrote: "I dare believe that in the mind of a competent Judge what I have performed will excite more surprise than what I have omitted to do, or failed in doing."

CHRISTOPHER MOORE

New York
1996

Lyric Poems

SONNET

TO THE AUTUMNAL MOON

Mild splendor of the various-vested Night!
　Mother of wildly-working visions! hail!
I watch thy gliding, while with watery light
　Thy weak eye glimmers through a fleecy veil;
And when thou lovest thy pale orb to shroud
　Behind the gather'd blackness lost on high;
And when thou dartest from the wind-rent cloud
　Thy placid lightning o'er the awaken'd sky.

Ah such is Hope! as changeful and as fair!
　Now dimly peering on the wistful sight;
Now hid behind the dragon-wing'd Despair:
　But soon emerging in her radiant might
She o'er the sorrow-clouded breast of Care
　Sails, like a meteor kindling in its flight.

QUAE NOCENT DOCENT

[IN CHRIST'S HOSPITAL BOOK]

O! mihi praeteritos referat si Jupiter annos!

Oh! might my ill-past hours return again!
No more, as then, should Sloth around me throw
    Her soul-enslaving, leaden chain!
No more the precious time would I employ
In giddy revels, or in thoughtless joy,
A present joy producing future woe.

But o'er the midnight Lamp I'd love to pore,
I'd seek with care fair Learning's depths to sound,
    And gather scientific Lore:
Or to mature the embryo thoughts inclin'd,
That half-conceiv'd lay struggling in my mind,
The cloisters' solitary gloom I'd round.

'Tis vain to wish, for Time has ta'en his flight—
For follies past be ceas'd the fruitless tears:
    Let follies past to future care incite.
Averse maturer judgments to obey
Youth owns, with pleasure owns, the Passions' sway,
But sage Experience only comes with years.

SONNET

TO THE RIVER OTTER

Dear native Brook! wild Streamlet of the West!
   How many various-fated years have past,
   What happy and what mournful hours, since last
I skimm'd the smooth thin stone along thy breast,
Numbering its light leaps! yet so deep imprest
Sink the sweet scenes of childhood, that mine eyes
   I never shut amid the sunny ray,
But straight with all their tints thy waters rise,
   Thy crossing plank, thy marge with willows gray,
And bedded sand that vein'd with various dyes
Gleam'd through thy bright transparence! On my way,
   Visions of Childhood! oft have ye beguil'd
Lone manhood's cares, yet waking fondest sighs:
   Ah! that once more I were a careless Child!

PANTISOCRACY

No more my visionary soul shall dwell
On joys that were; no more endure to weigh
The shame and anguish of the evil day,
Wisely forgetful! O'er the ocean swell
Sublime of Hope, I seek the cottag'd dell
Where Virtue calm with careless step may stray,
And dancing to the moonlight roundelay,
The wizard Passions weave an holy spell.
Eyes that have ach'd with Sorrow! Ye shall weep
Tears of doubt-mingled joy, like theirs who start
From Precipices of distemper'd sleep,
On which the fierce-eyed Fiends their revels keep,
And see the rising Sun, and feel it dart
New rays of pleasance trembling to the heart.

TO A YOUNG ASS

Poor little Foal of an oppresséd race!
I love the languid patience of thy face:
And oft with gentle hand I give thee bread,
And clap thy ragged coat, and pat thy head.
But what thy dulled spirits hath dismay'd,
That never thou dost sport along the glade?
And (most unlike the nature of things young)
That earthward still thy moveless head is hung?
Do thy prophetic fears anticipate,
Meek Child of Misery! thy future fate?
The starving meal, and all the thousand aches
"Which patient Merit of the Unworthy takes?"
Or is thy sad heart thrill'd with filial pain
To see thy wretched mother's shorten'd chain?
And truly, very piteous is *her* lot—
Chain'd to a log within a narrow spot,
Where the close-eaten grass is scarcely seen,
While sweet around her waves the tempting green!

Poor Ass! thy master should have learnt to show
Pity—best taught by fellowship of Woe!
For much I fear me that *He* lives like thee,
Half-famish'd in a land of Luxury!
How *askingly* its footsteps hither bend?
It seems to say, "And have I then one friend?"
Innocent foal! thou poor despis'd forlorn!
I hail thee *Brother*—spite of the fool's scorn!
And fain would take thee with me, in the Dell
Where high-soul'd Pantisocracy shall dwell!
Where Mirth shall tickle Plenty's ribless side,

And smiles from Beauty's Lip on sunbeams glide,
Where Toil shall wed young Health that charming Lass!
And use his sleek cows for a looking-glass—
Where Rats shall mess with Terriers hand-in-glove
And Mice with Pussy's Whiskers sport in Love
How thou wouldst toss thy heels in gamesome play,
And frisk about, as lamb or kitten gay!
Yea! and more musically sweet to me
Thy dissonant harsh bray of joy would be,
Than warbled melodies that soothe to rest
The aching of pale Fashion's vacant breast!

THE EOLIAN HARP

Composed at Clevedon, Somersetshire

My pensive Sara! thy soft cheek reclined
Thus on mine arm, most soothing sweet it is
To sit beside our Cot, our Cot o'ergrown
With white-flower'd Jasmin, and the broad-leav'd Myrtle,
(Meet emblems they of Innocence and Love!)
And watch the clouds, that late were rich with light,
Slow saddening round, and mark the star of eve
Serenely brilliant (such should Wisdom be)
Shine opposite! How exquisite the scents
Snatch'd from yon bean field! and the world *so* hush'd!
The stilly murmur of the distant Sea
Tells us of silence.
            And that simplest Lute,
Placed length-ways in the clasping casement, hark!
How by the desultory breeze caress'd,
Like some coy maid half-yielding to her lover,
It pours such sweet upbraiding, as must needs
Tempt to repeat the wrong! And now, its strings
Boldlier swept, the long sequacious notes
Over delicious surges sink and rise,
Such a soft floating witchery of sound
As twilight Elfins make, when they at eve
Voyage on gentle gales from Fairyland,
Where Melodies round honey-dropping flowers,
Footless and wild, like birds of Paradise,
Nor pause, nor perch, hovering on untam'd wing!
O! the one Life within us and abroad,
Which meets all motion and becomes its soul,
A light in sound, a sound-like power in light,
Rhythm in all thought, and joyance everywhere—

Methinks, it should have been impossible
Not to love all things in a world so fill'd;
Where the breeze warbles, and the mute still air
Is Music slumbering on her instrument.

　　And thus, my Love! as on the midway slope
Of yonder hill I stretch my limbs at noon,
Whilst through my half-clos'd eyelids I behold
The sunbeams dance, like diamonds, on the main,
And tranquil muse upon tranquillity;
Full many a thought uncall'd and undetain'd,
And many idle flitting fantasies,
Traverse my indolent and passive brain,
As wild and various as the random gales
That swell and flutter on this subject Lute!
　　And what if all of animated nature
Be but organic Harps diversely fram'd,
That tremble into thought, as o'er them sweeps
Plastic and vast, one intellectual breeze,
At once the Soul of each, and God of all?
　　But thy more serious eye a mild reproof
Darts, O belovéd Woman! nor such thoughts
Dim and unhallow'd dost thou not reject,
And biddest me walk humbly with my God.
Meek Daughter in the family of Christ!
Well hast thou said and holily disprais'd
These shapings of the unregenerate mind;
Bubbles that glitter as they rise and break
On vain Philosophy's aye-babbling spring.
For never guiltless may I speak of him,
The Incomprehensible! save when with awe
I praise him, and with Faith that inly *feels;*
Who with his saving mercies healéd me,
A sinful and most miserable man,
Wilder'd and dark, and gave me to possess
Peace, and this Cot, and thee, heart-honor'd Maid!

REFLECTIONS ON HAVING LEFT
A PLACE OF RETIREMENT

Sermoni propriora.—HORACE

Low was our pretty Cot: our tallest Rose
Peep'd at the chamber window. We could hear
At silent noon, and eve, and early morn,
The Sea's faint murmur. In the open air
Our Myrtles blossom'd; and across the porch
Thick Jasmins twined: the Little landscape round
Was green and woody, and refresh'd the eye.
It was a spot which you might aptly call
The Valley of Seclusion! Once I saw
(Hallowing his Sabbath Day by quietness)
A wealthy son of Commerce saunter by,
Bristowa's citizen: methought, it calm'd
His thirst of idle gold, and made him muse
With wiser feelings: for he paus'd, and look'd
With a pleased sadness, and gazed all around,
Then eyed our Cottage, and gazed round again,
And sighed, and said, it was a Blesséd Place.
And we *were* bless'd. Oft with patient ear
Long-listening to the viewless skylark's note
(Viewless, or haply for a moment seen
Gleaming on sunny wings) in whisper'd tones
I've said to my Belovéd, "Such, sweet Girl!
The inobtrusive song of Happiness,
Unearthly minstrelsy! then only heard
When the Soul seeks to hear; when all is hush'd,
And the Heart listens!"

But the time, when first
From that low Dell, steep up the stony Mount

I climb'd with perilous toil and reach'd the top,
Oh! what a goodly scene! *Here* the bleak mount,
The bare bleak mountain speckled thin with sheep;
Gray clouds, that shadowing spot the sunny fields;
And river, now with bushy rocks o'er-brow'd,
Now winding bright and full, with naked banks;
And seats, and lawns, the Abbey and the wood,
And cots, and hamlets, and faint city-spire;
The Channel *there*, the Islands and white sails,
Dim coasts, and cloud-like hills, and shoreless Ocean—
It seem'd like Omnipresence! God, methought,
Had built him there a Temple: the whole World
Seem'd *imag'd* in its vast circumference:
No *wish* profan'd my overwhelméd heart.
Blest hour! It was a luxury—to be!

    Ah! quiet Dell! dear Cot, and Mount sublime!
I was constrain'd to quit you. Was it right,
While my unnumber'd brethren toil'd and bled,
That I should dream away the entrusted hours
On rose-leaf beds, pampering the coward heart
With feelings all too delicate for use?
Sweet is the tear that from some Howard's eye
Drops on the cheek of one he lifts from earth:
And he that works me good with unmov'd face,
Does it but half: he chills me while he aids,
My benefactor, not my brother man!
Yet even this, this cold beneficence
Praise, praise it, O my Soul! oft as thou scann'st
The sluggard Pity's vision-weaving tribe!
Who sigh for Wretchedness, yet shun the Wretched,
Nursing in some delicious solitude
Their slothful loves and dainty sympathies!
I therefore go, and join head, heart, and hand,
Active and firm, to fight the bloodless fight
Of Science, Freedom, and the Truth in Christ.

Yet oft when after honorable toil
Rests the tir'd mind, and waking loves to dream,
My spirit shall revisit thee, dear Cot!
Thy Jasmin and thy window-peeping Rose,
And Myrtles fearless of the mild sea air.
And I shall sigh fond wishes—sweet Abode!
Ah!—had none greater! And that all had such!
It might be so—but the time is not yet.
Speed it, O Father! Let thy Kingdom come!

TO A YOUNG FRIEND

ON HIS PROPOSING TO DOMESTICATE
WITH THE AUTHOR

A mount, not wearisome and bare and steep,
   But a green mountain variously up-piled,
Where o'er the jutting rocks soft mosses creep,
Or color'd lichens with slow oozing weep;
   Where cypress and the darker yew start wild;
And, 'mid the summer torrents gentle dash
Dance brighten'd the red clusters of the ash;
   Beneath whose boughs, by those still sounds beguil'd,
Calm Pensiveness might muse herself to sleep;
   Till haply startled by some fleecy dam,
That rustling on the bushy cliff above
With melancholy bleat of anxious love,
   Made meek enquiry for her wandering lamb:
   Such a green mountain 'twere most sweet to climb,
E'en while the bosom ach'd with loneliness—
How more than sweet, if some dear friend should bless
   The adventurous toil, and up the path sublime
Now lead, now follow: the glad landscape round,
Wide and more wide, increasing without bound!

   O then 'twere loveliest sympathy, to mark
The berries of the half-uprooted ash
Dripping and bright; and list the torrent's dash—
   Beneath the cypress, or the yew more dark,
Seated at ease, on some smooth mossy rock;
In social silence now, and now to unlock
The treasur'd heart; arm linked in friendly arm,
Save if the one, his muse's witching charm
Muttering brow-bent, at unwatch'd distance lag;

Till high o'er head his beckoning friend appears,
And from the forehead of the topmost crag
   Shouts eagerly: for haply *there* uprears
That shadowing Pine its old romantic limbs,
   Which latest shall detain the enamor'd sight
Seen from below, when eve the valley dims,
   Tinged yellow with the rich departing light;
   And haply, bason'd in some unsunn'd cleft,
A beauteous spring, the rock's collected tears,
Sleeps shelter'd there, scarce wrinkled by the gale!
   Together thus, the world's vain turmoil left,
Stretch'd on the crag, and shadow'd by the pine,
   And bending o'er the clear delicious fount,
Ah! clearest youth! it were a lot divine
To cheat our noons in moralizing mood,
While west winds fann'd our temples toil-bedew'd:
   Then downwards slope, oft pausing, from the mount,
To some lone mansion, in some woody dale,
Where smiling with blue eye, Domestic Bliss
Gives *this* the Husband's, *that* the Brother's kiss!

   Thus rudely vers'd in allegoric lore,
The Hill of Knowledge I essayed to trace;
That verdurous hill with many a resting place,
And many a stream, whose warbling waters pour
   To glad, and fertilize the subject plains;
That hill with secret springs, and nooks untrod,
And many a fancy-blest and holy sod
   Where Inspiration, his diviner strains
Low-murmuring, lay; and starting from the rock's
Stiff evergreens, (whose spreading foliage mocks
Want's barren soil, and the bleak frosts of age,
And Bigotry's mad fire-invoking rage!)
O meek retiring spirit! we will climb,
Cheering and cheered, this lovely hill sublime;
   And from the stirring world uplifted high

(Whose noises, faintly wafted on the wind,
To quiet musings shall attune the mind,
   And oft the melancholy *theme* supply),
   There, while the prospect through the gazing eye
   Pours all its healthful greenness on the soul,
We'll smile at wealth, and learn to smile at fame,
Our hopes, our knowledge, and our joys the same,
   As neighboring fountains image each the whole:
Then when the mind hath drunk its fill of truth
   We'll discipline the heart to pure delight,
Rekindling sober joy's domestic flame.
They whom I love shall love thee, honor'd youth!
   Now may Heaven realize this vision bright!

ADDRESSED TO A YOUNG MAN
OF FORTUNE

WHO ABANDONED HIMSELF TO AN INDOLENT
AND CAUSELESS MELANCHOLY

[C. Lloyd]

Hence that fantastic wantonness of woe,
   O Youth to partial Fortune vainly dear!
To plunder'd Want's half-shelter'd hovel go,
   Go, and some hunger-bitten infant hear
   Moan haply in a dying mother's ear:
Or when the cold and dismal fog damps brood
O'er the rank churchyard with sear elm leaves strew'd,
Pace round some widow's grave, whose dearer part
   Was slaughter'd, where o'er his uncoffin'd limbs
The flocking flesh-birds scream'd! Then, while thy heart
   Groans, and thine eye a fiercer sorrow dims,
Know (and the truth shall kindle thy young mind)
What Nature makes thee mourn, she bids thee heal!
   O abject! if, to sickly dreams resign'd,
All effortless thou leave Life's commonweal
   A prey to Tyrants, Murderers of Mankind.

TO THE REV. GEORGE COLERIDGE

OF OTTERY ST. MARY, DEVON

With some poems

Notus in fratres animi paterni.
Horace, *Carmina,* II, 2

A blesséd lot hath he, who having passed
His youth and early manhood in the stir
And turmoil of the world, retreats at length,
With cares that move—not agitate the heart,
To the same dwelling where his father dwelt;
And haply views his tottering little ones
Embrace those agéd knees and climb that lap,
On which first kneeling his own infancy
Lisp'd its brief prayer. Such, O my earliest Friend!
Thy lot, and such thy brothers too enjoy.
At distance did ye climb Life's upland road,
Yet cheer'd and cheering: now fraternal love
Hath drawn you to one center. Be your days
Holy, and blest and blessing may ye live!

To me the Eternal Wisdom hath dispens'd
A different fortune and more different mind—
Me from the spot where first I sprang to light
Too soon transplanted, ere my soul had fix'd
Its first domestic loves; and hence through life
Chasing chance-started friendships. A brief while
Some have preserv'd me from life's pelting ills;
But, like a tree with leaves of feeble stem,
If the clouds lasted, and a sudden breeze
Ruffled the boughs, they on my head at once
Dropped the collected shower; and some most false,
False and fair-foliag'd as the Manchineel,

Have tempted me to slumber in their shade
E'en mid the storm; then breathing subtlest damps,
Mix'd their own venom with the rain from Heaven,
That I woke poison'd! But, all praise to Him
Who gives us all things, more have yielded me
Permanent shelter; and beside one Friend,
Beneath the impervious covert of one oak,
I've rais'd a lowly shed, and know the names
Of Husband and of Father; not unhearing
Of that divine and nightly-whispering Voice,
Which from my childhood to maturer years
Spake to me of predestinated wreaths,
Bright with no fading colors!

                         Yet at times
My soul is sad, that I have roam'd through life
Still most a stranger, most with naked heart
At mine own home and birthplace: chiefly then,
When I remember thee, my earliest Friend!
Thee, who didst watch my boyhood and my youth;
Didst trace my wanderings with a father's eye;
And boding evil yet still hoping good,
Rebuk'd each fault, and over all my woes
Sorrow'd in silence! He who counts alone
The beatings of the solitary heart,
That Being knows, how I have lov'd thee ever,
Lov'd as a brother, as a son rever'd thee!
Oh! 'tis to me an ever new delight,
To talk of thee and thine: or when the blast
Of the shrill winter, rattling our rude sash,
Endears the cleanly hearth and social bowl;
Or when, as now, on some delicious eve,
We in our sweet sequester'd orchard plot
Sit on the tree crook'd earthward; whose old boughs,
That hang above us in an arborous roof,
Stirr'd by the faint gale of departing May,
Send their loose blossoms slanting o'er our heads!

Nor dost not thou sometimes recall those hours,
When with the joy of hope thou gavest thine ear
To my wild firstling-lays. Since then my song
Hath sounded deeper notes, such as beseem
Or that sad wisdom folly leaves behind,
Or such as, tuned to these tumultuous times,
Cope with the tempest's swell!

       These various strains,
Which I have fram'd in many a various mood,
Accept, my Brother! and (for some perchance
Will strike discordant on thy milder mind)
If aught of error or intemperate truth
Should meet thine ear, think thou that riper Age
Will calm it down, and let thy love forgive it!

NETHER-STOWEY, SOMERSET, MAY 26, 1797

THIS LIME-TREE BOWER MY PRISON

[ADDRESSED TO CHARLES LAMB, OF THE INDIA HOUSE, LONDON]

In the June of 1797 some long-expected friends paid a visit to the author's cottage; and on the morning of their arrival, he met with an accident, which disabled him from walking during the whole time of their stay. One evening, when they had left him for a few hours, he composed the following lines in the garden bower.

Well, they are gone, and here must I remain,
This lime-tree bower my prison! I have lost
Beauties and feelings, such as would have been
Most sweet to my remembrance even when age
Had dimm'd mine eyes to blindness! They, meanwhile,
Friends, whom I never more may meet again,
On springy heath, along the hilltop edge,
Wander in gladness, and wind down, perchance,
To that still roaring dell, of which I told;
The roaring dell, o'erwooded, narrow, deep,
And only speckled by the midday sun;
Where its slim trunk the ash from rock to rock
Flings arching like a bridge—that branchless ash,
Unsunn'd and damp, whose few poor yellow leaves
Ne'er tremble in the gale, yet tremble still,
Fann'd by the waterfall! and there my friends
Behold the dark green file of long lank weeds
That all at once (a most fantastic sight!)
Still nod and drip beneath the dripping edge
Of the blue clay-stone.

              Now, my friends emerge
Beneath the wide wide Heaven—and view again

The many-steepled tract magnificent
Of hilly fields and meadows, and the sea,
With some fair bark, perhaps, whose sails light up
The slip of smooth clear blue betwixt two Isles
Of purple shadow! Yes! they wander on
In gladness all; but thou, methinks, most glad,
My gentle-hearted Charles! for thou hast pined
And hunger'd after Nature, many a year,
In the great City pent, winning thy way
With sad yet patient soul, through evil and pain
And strange calamity! Ah! slowly sink
Behind the western ridge, thou glorious Sun!
Shine in the slant beams of the sinking orb,
Ye purple heath-flowers! richlier burn, ye clouds!
Live in the yellow light, ye distant groves!
And kindle, thou blue Ocean! So my friend
Struck with deep joy may stand, as I have stood,
Silent with swimming sense; yea, gazing round
On the wide landscape, gaze till all doth seem
Less gross than bodily; and of such hues
As veil the Almighty Spirit, when yet he makes
Spirits perceive his presence.

                    A delight
Comes sudden on my heart, and I am glad
As I myself were there! Nor in this bower,
This little lime-tree bower, have I not mark'd
Much that has sooth'd me. Pale beneath the blaze
Hung the transparent foliage; and I watch'd
Some broad and sunny leaf, and lov'd to see
The shadow of the leaf and stem above
Dappling its sunshine! And that walnut tree
Was richly ting'd, and a deep radiance lay
Full on the ancient ivy, which usurps
Those fronting elms, and now, with blackest mass
Makes their dark branches gleam a lighter hue
Through the late twilight: and though now the bat

Wheels silent by, and not a swallow twitters,
Yet still the solitary humble-bee
Sings in the bean-flower! Henceforth I shall know
That Nature ne'er deserts the wise and pure;
No plot so narrow, be but Nature there,
No waste so vacant, but may well employ
Each faculty of sense, and keep the heart
Awake to Love and Beauty! and sometimes
'Tis well to be bereft of promis'd good,
That we may lift the soul, and contemplate
With lively joy the joys we cannot share.
My gentle-hearted Charles! when the last rook
Beat its straight path along the dusky air
Homewards, I blest it! deeming its black wing
(Now a dim speck, now vanishing in light)
Had cross'd the mighty Orb's dilated glory,
While thou stood'st gazing; or, when all was still,
Flew creeking o'er thy head, and had a charm.
For thee, my gentle-hearted Charles, to whom
No sound is dissonant which tells of Life.

THE DUNGEON

[From *Osorio*, Act V; and *Remorse*, Act V, Scene i.]

And this place our forefathers made for man!
This is the process of our love and wisdom,
To each poor brother who offends against us—
Most innocent, perhaps—and what if guilty?
Is this the only cure? Merciful God!
Each pore and natural outlet shrivel'd up
By Ignorance and parching Poverty,
His energies roll back upon his heart,
And stagnate and corrupt; till chang'd to poison,
They break out on him, like a loathsome plague-spot;
Then we call in our pamper'd mountebanks—
And this is their best cure! uncomforted
And friendless solitude, groaning and tears,
And savage faces, at the clanking hour,
Seen through the steams and vapor of his dungeon,
By the lamp's dismal twilight! So he lies
Circled with evil, till his very soul
Unmolds its essence, hopelessly deform'd
By sights of evermore deformity!

With other ministrations thou, O Nature!
Healest thy wandering and distemper'd child:
Thou pourest on him thy soft influences,
Thy sunny hues, fair forms, and breathing sweets,
Thy melodies of woods, and winds, and waters,
Will he relent, and can no more endure
To be a jarring and a dissonant thing,
Amid this general dance and minstrelsy;
But, bursting into tears, wins back his way,
His angry spirit heal'd and harmoniz'd
By the benignant touch of Love and Beauty.

FROST AT MIDNIGHT

The Frost performs its secret ministry,
Unhelped by any wind. The owlet's cry
Came loud—and hark, again! loud as before.
The inmates of my Cottage, all at rest,
Have left me to that solitude, which suits
Abstruser musings: save that at my side
My cradled infant slumbers peacefully.
'Tis calm indeed! so calm, that it disturbs
And vexes meditation with its strange
And extreme silentness. Sea, hill, and wood,
This populous village! Sea, and hill, and wood,
With all the numberless goings-on of life,
Inaudible as dreams! the thin blue flame
Lies on my low-burnt fire, and quivers not;
Only that film, which fluttered on the grate,
Still flutters there, the sole unquiet thing.
Methinks, its motion in this hush of nature
Gives it dim sympathies with me who live,
Making it a companionable form,
Whose puny flaps and freaks the idling Spirit
By its own moods interprets, everywhere
Echo or mirror seeking of itself,
And makes a toy of Thought.

                              But O! how oft,
How oft, at school, with most believing mind,
Presageful, have I gazed upon the bars,
To watch that fluttering *stranger?* and as oft
With unclosed lids, already had I dreamt
Of my sweet birthplace, and the old church tower,
Whose bells, the poor man's only music, rang

From morn to evening, all the hot Fair-day,
So sweetly, that they stirred and haunted me
With a wild pleasure, falling on mine ear
Most like articulate sounds of things to come!
So gazed I, till the soothing things, I dreamt,
Lulled me to sleep, and sleep prolonged my dreams!
And so I brooded all the following morn,
Awed by the stern preceptor's face, mine eye
Fixed with mock study on my swimming book:
Save if the door half-opened, and I snatched
A hasty glance, and still my heart leaped up,
For still I hoped to see the *stranger's* face,
Townsman, or aunt, or sister more beloved,
My playmate when we both were clothed alike!

Dear Babe, that sleepest cradled by my side,
Whose gentle breathings, heard in this deep calm,
Fill up the intersperséd vacancies
And momentary pauses of the thought!
My babe so beautiful! it thrills my heart
With tender gladness, thus to look at thee,
And think that thou shalt learn far other lore,
And in far other scenes! For I was reared
In the great city, pent 'mid cloisters dim,
And saw naught lovely but the sky and stars.
But *thou,* my babe! shalt wander like a breeze
By lakes and sandy shores, beneath the crags
Of ancient mountain, and beneath the clouds,
Which image in their bulk both lakes and shores
And mountain crags: so shalt thou see and hear
The lovely shapes and sounds intelligible
Of that eternal language, which thy God
Utters, who from eternity doth teach
Himself in all, and all things in himself.
Great universal Teacher! he shall mold
Thy spirit, and by giving make it ask.

Therefore all seasons shall be sweet to thee,
Whether the summer clothe the general earth
With greenness, or the redbreast sit and sing
Betwixt the tufts of snow on the bare branch
Of mossy apple tree, while the nigh thatch
Smokes in the sun-thaw; whether the eave-drops fall
Heard only in the trances of the blast,
Or if the secret ministry of frost
Shall hang them up in silent icicles,
Quietly shining to the quiet Moon.

FRANCE: AN ODE

ARGUMENT

"First Stanza. *An invocation to those objects in Nature the contemplation of which had inspired the Poet with a devotional love of Liberty.* Second Stanza. *The exultation of the Poet at the commencement of the French Revolution, and his unqualified abhorrence of the Alliance against the Republic.* Third Stanza. *The blasphemies and horrors during the domination of the Terrorists regarded by the Poet as a transient storm, and as the natural consequence of the former despotism and of the foul superstition of Popery. Reason, indeed, began to suggest many apprehensions; yet still the Poet struggled to retain the hope that France would make conquests by no other means than by presenting to the observation of Europe a people more happy and better instructed than under other forms of Government.* Fourth Stanza, *Switzerland, and the Poet's recantation.* Fifth Stanza. *An address to Liberty, in which the Poet expresses his conviction that those feelings and that grand ideal of Freedom which the mind attains by its contemplation of its individual nature, and of the sublime surrounding objects (see Stanza the First) do not belong to men, as a society, nor can possibly be either gratified or realized, under any form of human government; but belong to the individual man, so far as he is pure, and inflamed with the love and adoration of God in Nature.*"

I

Ye Clouds! that far above me float and pause,
   Whose pathless march no mortal may control!
   Ye Ocean Waves! that, wheresoe'er ye roll,

Yield homage only to eternal laws!
Ye Woods! that listen to the night-birds singing,
   Midway the smooth and perilous slope reclined,
Save when your own imperious branches swinging,
   Have made a solemn music of the wind!
Where, like a man beloved of God,
Through glooms, which never woodman trod,
   How oft, pursuing fancies holy,
My moonlight way o'er flowering weeds I wound,
   Inspired, beyond the guess of folly,
By each rude shape and wild unconquerable sound!
O ye loud Waves! and O ye Forests high!
   And O ye Clouds that far above me soared!
Thou rising Sun! thou blue rejoicing Sky!
   Yea, everything that is and will be free!
   Bear witness for me, wheresoe'er ye be,
   With what deep worship I have still adored
     The spirit of divinest Liberty.

II

When France in wrath her giant limbs upreared,
   And with that oath, which smote air, earth, and sea,
   Stamped her strong foot and said she would be free,
Bear witness for me, how I hoped and feared!
With what a joy my lofty gratulation
   Unawed I sang, amid a slavish band:
And when to whelm the disenchanted nation,
   Like fiends embattled by a wizard's wand,
     The Monarchs marched in evil day,
     And Britain joined the dire array;
   Though dear her shores and circling ocean,
Though many friendships, many youthful loves
   Had swoln the patriot emotion
And flung a magic light o'er all her hills and groves;
Yet still my voice, unaltered, sang defeat
   To all that braved the tyrant-quelling lance,

And shame too long delayed and vain retreat!
For ne'er, O Liberty! with partial aim
I dimmed thy light or damped thy holy flame;
   But blessed the paeans of delivered France,
And hung my head and wept at Britain's name.

III

"And what," I said, "though Blasphemy's loud scream
   With that sweet music of deliverance strove!
   Though all the fierce and drunken passions wove
A dance more wild than e'er was maniac's dream!
   Ye storms, that round the dawning East assembled,
The Sun was rising, though ye hid his light!"
   And when, to soothe my soul, that hoped and
         trembled,
The dissonance ceased, and all seemed calm and
         bright;
   When France her front deep-scarr'd and gory
   Concealed with clustering wreaths of glory;
      When, insupportably advancing,
Her arm made mockery of the warrior's ramp;
      While timid looks of fury glancing,
   Domestic treason, crushed beneath her fatal stamp,
Writhed like a wounded dragon in his gore;
   Then I reproached my fears that would not flee;
"And soon," I said, "shall Wisdom teach her lore
In the low huts of them that toil and groan!
And, conquering by her happiness alone,
   Shall France compel the nations to be free,
Till Love and Joy look round, and call the Earth their
      own."

IV

Forgive me, Freedom! O forgive those dreams!
   I hear thy voice, I hear thy loud lament,
   From bleak Helvetia's icy caverns sent—

I hear thy groans upon her bloodstained streams!
   Heroes, that for your peaceful country perished,
And ye that, fleeing, spot your mountain snows
   With bleeding wounds; forgive me, that I cherished
One thought that ever blessed your cruel foes!
   To scatter rage, and traitorous guilt,
   Where Peace her jealous home had built;
     A patriot-race to disinherit
Of all that made their stormy wilds so dear;
     And with inexpiable spirit
To taint the bloodless freedom of the mountaineer—
O France, that mockest Heaven, adulterous, blind,
   And patriot only in pernicious toils!
Are these thy boasts, Champion of human kind?
   To mix with Kings in the low lust of sway,
Yell in the hunt, and share the murderous prey;
To insult the shrine of Liberty with spoils
   From freemen torn; to tempt and to betray?

V

   The Sensual and the Dark rebel in vain,
   Slaves by their own compulsion! In mad game
   They burst their manacles and wear the name
     Of Freedom, graven on a heavier chain!
   O Liberty! with profitless endeavor
Have I pursued thee, many a weary hour;
   But thou nor swell'st the victor's strain, nor ever
Didst breathe thy soul in forms of human power.
   Alike from all, howe'er they praise thee,
   (Nor prayer, nor boastful name delays thee)
     Alike from Priestcraft's harpy minions,
   And factious Blasphemy's obscener slaves,
     Thou speedest on thy subtle pinions,
The guide of homeless winds, and playmate of the
     waves!

And there I felt thee!—on that sea cliff's verge,
    Whose pines, scarce traveled by the breeze above,
Had made one murmur with the distant surge!
Yes; while I stood and gazed, my temples bare,
And shot my being through earth, sea, and air,
    Possessing all things with intensest love,
      O Liberty! my spirit felt thee there.

LEWTI

OR THE CIRCASSIAN LOVE-CHAUNT

At midnight by the stream I roved,
To forget the form I loved.
Image of Lewti! from my mind
Depart; for Lewti is not kind.

The Moon was high, the moonlight gleam
   And the shadow of a star
Heaved upon Tamaha's stream;
   But the rock shone brighter far,
The rock half-sheltered from my view
By pendent boughs of tressy yew—
So shines my Lewti's forehead fair,
Gleaming through her sable hair,
Image of Lewti! from my mind
Depart; for Lewti is not kind.

I saw a cloud of palest hue,
   Onward to the moon it passed;
Still brighter and more bright it grew,
With floating colors not a few,
Till it reached the moon at last:
Then the cloud was wholly bright,
With a rich and amber light!
And so with many a hope I seek,
   And with such joy I find my Lewti;
And even so my pale wan cheek
   Drinks in as deep a flush of beauty!
Nay, treacherous image! leave my mind,
If Lewti never will be kind.

The little cloud—it floats away,
    Away it goes; away so soon!
Alas! it has no power to stay:
Its hues are dim, its hues are gray—
    Away it passes from the moon!
How mournfully it seems to fly,
    Ever fading more and more,
To joyless regions of the sky—
    And now 'tis whiter than before!
As white as my poor cheek will be,
    When, Lewti! on my couch I lie,
A dying man for love of thee.
Nay, treacherous image! leave my mind—
And yet, thou didst not look unkind.

I saw a vapor in the sky,
Thin, and white, and very high;
I ne'er beheld so thin a cloud:
    Perhaps the breezes that can fly
    Now below and now above,
Have snatched aloft the lawny shroud.
    Of Lady fair—that died for love.
For maids, as well as youths, have perished
From fruitless love too fondly cherished.
Nay, treacherous image! leave my mind—
For Lewti never will be kind.

Hush! my heedless feet from under
    Slip the crumbling banks forever:
Like echoes to a distant thunder,
    They plunge into the gentle river.
The river swans have heard my tread,
And startle from their reedy bed.
O beauteous birds! methinks ye measure
    Your movements to some heavenly tune!
O beauteous birds! 'tis such a pleasure

To see you move beneath the moon,
I would it were your true delight
To sleep by day and wake all night.

I know the place where Lewti lies,
When silent night has closed her eyes:
    It is a breezy jasmine-bower,
The nightingale sings o'er her head:
    Voice of the Night! had I the power
That leafy labyrinth to thread,
    And creep, like thee, with soundless tread,
I then might view her bosom white
Heaving lovely to my sight,
As these two swans together heave
On the gently-swelling wave.

Oh! that she saw me in a dream,
    And dreamt that I had died for care;
All pale and wasted I would seem,
    Yet fair withal, as spirits are!
I'd die indeed, if I might see
Her bosom heave, and heave for me!
Soothe, gentle image! soothe my mind!
Tomorrow Lewti may be kind.

FEARS IN SOLITUDE

WRITTEN IN APRIL 1798, DURING ALARM OF AN INVASION

A green and silent spot, amid the hills,
A small and silent dell! O'er stiller place
No singing skylark ever poised himself.
The hills are heathy, save that swelling slope,
Which hath a gay and gorgeous covering on,
All golden with the never-bloomless furze,
Which now blooms most profusely: but the dell,
Bathed by the mist, is fresh and delicate
As vernal cornfield, or the unripe flax,
When, through its half-transparent stalks, at eve,
The level sunshine glimmers with green light.
Oh! 'tis a quiet spirit-healing nook!
Which all, methinks, would love; but chiefly he,
The humble man, who, in his youthful years,
Knew just so much of folly, as had made
His early manhood more securely wise!
Here he might lie on fern or withered heath,
While from the singing lark (that sings unseen
The minstrelsy that solitude loves best),
And from the sun, and from the breezy air,
Sweet influences trembled o'er his frame;
And he, with many feelings, many thoughts,
Made up a meditative joy, and found
Religious meanings in the forms of Nature!
And so, his senses gradually wrapt
In a half sleep, he dreams of better worlds,
And dreaming hears thee still, O singing lark,
That singest like an angel in the clouds!

My God! it is a melancholy thing
For such a man, who would full fain preserve
His soul in calmness, yet perforce must feel
For all his human brethren—O my God!
It weighs upon the heart, that he must think
What uproar and what strife may now be stirring
This way or that way o'er these silent hills—
Invasion, and the thunder and the shout,
And all the crash of onset; fear and rage,
And undetermined conflict—even now,
Even now, perchance, and in his native isle:
Carnage and groans beneath this blessed sun!
We have offended, Oh! my countrymen!
We have offended very grievously,
And been most tyrannous. From east to west
A groan of accusation pierces Heaven!
The wretched plead against us; multitudes
Countless and vehement, the sons of God,
Our brethren! Like a cloud that travels on,
Steamed up from Cairo's swamps of pestilence,
Even so, my countrymen! have we gone forth
And borne to distant tribes slavery and pangs,
And, deadlier far, our vices, whose deep taint
With slow perdition murders the whole man,
His body and his soul! Meanwhile, at home,
All individual dignity and power
Engulfed in Courts, Committees, Institutions,
Associations and Societies,
A vain, speech-mouthing, speech-reporting Guild,
One Benefit-Club for mutual flattery,
We have drunk up, demure as at a grace,
Pollutions from the brimming cup of wealth;
Contemptuous of all honorable rule,
Yet bartering freedom and the poor man's life
For gold, as at a market! The sweet words
Of Christian promise, words that even yet

Might stem destruction, were they wisely preached,
Are muttered o'er by men, whose tones proclaim
How flat and wearisome they feel their trade:
Rank scoffers some, but most too indolent
To deem them falsehoods or to know their truth.
Oh! blasphemous! the Book of Life is made
A superstitious instrument, on which
We gabble o'er the oaths we mean to break;
For all must swear—all and in every place,
College and wharf, council and justice-court;
All, all must swear, the briber and the bribed;
Merchant and lawyer, senator and priest,
The rich, the poor, the old man and the young;
All, all make up one scheme of perjury,
That faith doth reel; the very name of God
Sounds like a juggler's charm; and, bold with joy,
Forth from his dark and lonely hiding place,
(Portentous sight!) the owlet Atheism,
Sailing on obscene wings athwart the noon,
Drops his blue-fringéd lids, and holds them close,
And hooting at the glorious sun in Heaven,
Cries out, "Where is it?"

                     Thankless too for peace,
(Peace long preserved by fleets and perilous seas)
Secure from actual warfare, we have loved
To swell the war-whoop, passionate for war!
Alas! for ages ignorant of all
Its ghastlier workings (famine or blue plague,
Battle, or siege, or flight through wintry snows),
We, this whole people, have been clamorous
For war and bloodshed; animating sports,
The which we pay for as a thing to talk of,
Spectators and not combatants! No guess
Anticipative of a wrong unfelt,
No speculation on contingency,

However dim and vague, too vague and dim
To yield a justifying cause; and forth,
(Stuffed out with big preamble, holy names,
And adjurations of the God in Heaven,)
We send our mandates for the certain death
Of thousands and ten thousands! Boys and girls,
And women, that would groan to see a child
Pull off an insect's leg, all read of war,
The best amusement for our morning meal!
The poor wretch, who has learnt his only prayers
From curses, who knows scarcely words enough
To ask a blessing from his Heavenly Father,
Becomes a fluent phraseman, absolute
And technical in victories and defeats,
And all our dainty terms for fratricide;
Terms which we trundle smoothly o'er our tongues
Like mere abstractions, empty sounds to which
We join no feeling and attach no form!
As if the soldier died without a wound;
As if the fibers of this godlike frame
Were gored without a pang; as if the wretch,
Who fell in battle, doing bloody deeds,
Passed off to Heaven, translated and not killed;
As though he had no wife to pine for him,
No God to judge him! Therefore, evil days
Are coming on us, O my countrymen!
And what if all-avenging Providence,
Strong and retributive, should make us know
The meaning of our words, force us to feel
The desolation and the agony
Of our fierce doings?

              Spare us yet awhile,
Father and God! O! spare us yet awhile!
Oh! let not English women drag their flight
Fainting beneath the burthen of their babes,

Of the sweet infants, that but yesterday
Laughed at the breast! Sons, brothers, husbands, all
Who ever gazed with fondness on the forms
Which grew up with you round the same fireside,
And all who ever heard the sabbath bells
Without the infidel's scorn, make yourselves pure!
Stand forth! be men! repel an impious foe,
Impious and false, a light yet cruel race,
Who laugh away all virtue, mingling mirth
With deeds of murder; and still promising
Freedom, themselves too sensual to be free,
Poison life's amities, and cheat the heart
Of faith and quiet hope, and all that soothes,
And all that lifts the spirit! Stand we forth;
Render them back upon the insulted ocean,
And let them toss as idly on its waves
As the vile seaweed, which some mountain-blast
Swept from our shores! And oh! may we return
Not with a drunken triumph, but with fear,
Repenting of the wrongs with which we stung
So fierce a foe to frenzy!

                    I have told,
O Britons! O my brethren! I have told
Most bitter truth, but without bitterness.
Nor deem my zeal or factious or mistimed;
For never can true courage dwell with them,
Who, playing tricks with conscience, dare not look
At their own vices. We have been too long
Dupes of a deep delusion! Some, belike,
Groaning with restless enmity, expect
All change from change of constituted power;
As if a Government had been a robe,
On which our vice and wretchedness were tagged
Like fancy-points and fringes, with the robe
Pulled off at pleasure. Fondly these attach

A radical causation to a few
Poor drudges of chastising Providence,
Who borrow all their hues and qualities
From our own folly and rank wickedness,
Which gave them birth and nursed them. Others,
      meanwhile,
Dote with a mad idolatry; and all
Who will not fall before their images,
And yield them worship, they are enemies
Even of their country!

                 Such have I been deemed—
But, O dear Britain! O my Mother Isle!
Needs must thou prove a name most dear and holy
To me, a son, a brother, and a friend,
A husband, and a father! who revere
All bonds of natural love, and find them all
Within the limits of thy rocky shores.
O native Britain! O my Mother Isle!
How shouldst thou prove aught else but dear and holy
To me, who from thy lakes and mountain-hills,
Thy clouds, thy quiet dales, thy rocks and seas,
Have drunk in all my intellectual life,
All sweet sensations, all ennobling thoughts,
All adoration of the God in nature,
All lovely and all honorable things,
Whatever makes this mortal spirit feel
The joy and greatness of its future being?
There lives nor form nor feeling in my soul
Unborrowed from my country! O divine
And beauteous island! thou hast been my sole
And most magnificent temple, in the which
I walk with awe, and sing my stately songs,
Loving the God that made me!—

                 May my fears,
My filial fears, be vain! and may the vaunts

And menace of the vengeful enemy
Pass like the gust, that roared and died away
In the distant tree: which heard, and only heard
In this low dell, bowed not the delicate grass.

But now the gentle dew-fall sends abroad
The fruit-like perfume of the golden furze:
The light has left the summit of the hill,
Though still a sunny gleam lies beautiful
Aslant the ivied beacon. Now farewell,
Farewell, awhile, O soft and silent spot!
On the green sheep track, up the heathy hill,
Homeward I wind my way; and lo! recalled
From bodings that have well-nigh wearied me,
I find myself upon the brow, and pause
Startled! And after lonely sojourning
In such a quiet and surrounded nook,
This burst of prospect, here the shadowy main,
Dim-tinted, there the mighty majesty
Of that huge amphitheater of rich
And elmy fields, seems like society—
Conversing with the mind, and giving it
A livelier impulse and a dance of thought!
And now, belovéd Stowey! I behold
Thy church tower, and, methinks, the four huge elms
Clustering, which mark the mansion of my friend;
And close behind them, hidden from my view,
Is my own lowly cottage, where my babe
And my babe's mother dwell in peace! With light
And quickened footsteps thitherward I tend,
Remembering thee, O green and silent dell!
And grateful, that by nature's quietness
And solitary musings, all my heart
Is softened, and made worthy to indulge
Love, and the thoughts that yearn for human kind.

THE NIGHTINGALE

A CONVERSATION POEM, APRIL 1798

No cloud, no relique of the sunken day
Distinguishes the West, no long thin slip
Of sullen light, no obscure trembling hues.
Come, we will rest on this old mossy bridge!
You see the glimmer of the stream beneath,
But hear no murmuring: it flows silently,
O'er its soft bed of verdure. All is still,
A balmy night! and though the stars be dim,
Yet let us think upon the vernal showers
That gladden the green earth, and we shall find
A pleasure in the dimness of the stars.
And hark! the Nightingale begins its song,
"Most musical, most melancholy" bird!
A melancholy bird? Oh! idle thought!
In Nature there is nothing melancholy.
But some night-wandering man whose heart was pierced
With the remembrance of a grievous wrong,
Or slow distemper, or neglected love,
(And so, poor wretch! filled all things with himself,
And made all gentle sounds tell back the tale
Of his own sorrow) he, and such as he,
First named these notes a melancholy strain.
And many a poet echoes the conceit;
Poet who hath been building up the rhyme
When he had better far have stretched his limbs
Beside a brook in mossy forest dell,
By sun or moonlight, to the influxes
Of shapes and sounds and shifting elements
Surrendering his whole spirit, of his song
And of his fame forgetful! so his fame

Should share in Nature's immortality,
A venerable thing! and so his song
Should make all Nature lovelier, and itself
Be loved like Nature! But 'twill not be so;
And youths and maidens most poetical,
Who lose the deepening twilights of the spring
In ballrooms and hot theaters, they still
Full of meek sympathy must heave their sighs
O'er Philomela's pity-pleading strains.

My Friend, and thou, our Sister! we have learnt
A different lore: we may not thus profane
Nature's sweet voices, always full of love
And joyance! 'Tis the merry Nightingale
That crowds, and hurries, and precipitates
With fast thick warble his delicious notes,
As he were fearful that an April night
Would be too short for him to utter forth
His love-chant, and disburthen his full soul
Of all its music!
        And I know a grove
Of large extent, hard by a castle huge,
Which the great lord inhabits not; and so
This grove is wild with tangling underwood,
And the trim walks are broken up, and grass,
Thin grass and king-cups grow within the paths.
But never elsewhere in one place I knew
So many nightingales; and far and near,
In wood and thicket, over the wide grove,
They answer and provoke each other's song,
With skirmish and capricious passagings,
And murmurs musical and swift jug jug,
And one low piping sound more sweet than all—
Stirring the air with such a harmony,
That should you close your eyes, you might almost
Forget it was not day! On moonlight bushes,

Whose dewy leaflets are but half-disclosed,
You may perchance behold them on the twigs,
Their bright, bright eyes, their eyes both bright and full,
Glistening, while many a glowworm in the shade
Lights up her love-torch.
                        A most gentle Maid,
Who dwelleth in her hospitable home
Hard by the castle, and at latest eve
(Even like a Lady vowed and dedicate
To something more than Nature in the grove)
Glides through the pathways; she knows all their notes,
That gentle Maid! and oft, a moment's space,
What time the moon was lost behind a cloud,
Hath heard a pause of silence; till the moon
Emerging, hath awakened earth and sky
With one sensation, and those wakeful birds
Have all burst forth in choral minstrelsy,
As if some sudden gale had swept at once
A hundred airy harps! And she hath watched
Many a nightingale perch giddily
On blossomy twig still swinging from the breeze,
And to that motion tune his wanton song
Like tipsy Joy that reels with tossing head.

Farewell, O Warbler! till tomorrow eve,
And you, my friends! farewell, a short farewell!
We have been loitering long and pleasantly,
And now for our dear homes—That strain again!
Full fain it would delay me! My dear babe,
Who, capable of no articulate sound,
Mars all things with his imitative lisp,
How he would place his hand beside his ear,
His little hand, the small forefinger up,
And bid us listen! And I deem it wise
To make him Nature's playmate. He knows well
The evening star; and once, when he awoke

In most distressful mood (some inward pain
Had made up that strange thing, an infant's dream—)
I hurried with him to our orchard plot,
And he beheld the moon, and, hushed at once,
Suspends his sobs, and laughs most silently,
While his fair eyes, that swam with undropped tears,
Did glitter in the yellow moonbeam! Well!—
It is a father's tale: But if that Heaven
Should give me life, his childhood shall grow up
Familiar with these songs, that with the night
He may associate joy—Once more, farewell,
Sweet Nightingale! Once more, my friends! Farewell.

KUBLA KHAN

OR, A VISION IN A DREAM

A FRAGMENT

The following fragment is here published at the request at a poet of great and deserved celebrity [Lord Byron], and, as far as the Author's own opinions are concerned, rather as a psychological curiosity, than on the ground of any supposed poetic merits.

In the summer of the year 1797, the Author, then in ill health, had retired to a lonely farmhouse between Porlock and Linton, on the Exmoor confines of Somerset and Devonshire. In consequence of a slight indisposition, an anodyne had been prescribed, from the effects of which he fell asleep in his chair at the moment that he was reading the following sentence, or words of the same substance, in "Purchas's Pilgrimage": "Here the Khan Kubla commanded a palace to be built, and a stately garden thereunto. And thus ten miles of fertile ground were inclosed with a wall." The Author continued for about three hours in a profound sleep, at least of the external senses, during which time he has the most vivid confidence, that he could not have composed less than from two to three hundred lines; if that indeed can be called composition in which all the images rose up before him as things, with a parallel production of the correspondent expressions, without any sensation or consciousness of effort. On awaking he appeared to himself to have a distinct recollection at the whole, and taking his pen, ink, and paper, instantly and eagerly wrote down the lines that are here preserved. At this moment he was unfortunately called out by a person on business from Porlock, and detained by him above an hour, and on his return to his room, found, to his no small surprise and mortification, that though he still retained some vague and dim recollection of the general purport of the vision, yet, with the exception of some eight or ten scattered lines and images, all the rest had passed away like the images on the surface of a stream into which a stone has been cast, but, alas! without the after restoration of the latter!

In Xanadu did Kubla Khan
A stately pleasure dome decree:
Where Alph, the sacred river, ran
Through caverns measureless to man
    Down to a sunless sea.
So twice five miles of fertile ground
With walls and towers were girdled round:
And there were gardens bright with sinuous rills,
Where blossomed many an incense-bearing tree;
And here were forests ancient as the hills,
Enfolding sunny spots of greenery.

But oh! that deep romantic chasm which slanted
Down the green hill athwart a cedarn cover!
A savage place! as holy and enchanted
As e'er beneath a waning moon was haunted
By woman wailing for her demon-lover!
And from this chasm, with ceaseless turmoil seething.
As if this earth in fast thick pants were breathing,
A mighty fountain momently was forced:
Amid whose swift half-intermitted burst
Huge fragments vaulted like rebounding hail,
Or chaffy grain beneath the thresher's flail:
And 'mid these dancing rocks at once and ever
It flung up momently the sacred river.
Five miles meandering with a mazy motion
Through wood and dale the sacred river ran,
Then reached the caverns measureless to man,
And sank in tumult to a lifeless ocean:
And 'mid this tumult Kubla heard from far
Ancestral voices prophesying war!
    The shadow of the dome of pleasure
    Floated midway on the waves;
    Where was heard the mingled measure
    From the fountain and the caves.
It was a miracle of rare device,
A sunny pleasure dome with caves of ice!

A damsel with a dulcimer
In a vision once I saw:
It was an Abyssinian maid,
And on her dulcimer she played,
Singing of Mount Abora.
Could I revive within me
Her symphony and song,
To such a deep delight 'twould win me,
That with music loud and long,
I would build that dome in air,
That sunny dome! those caves of ice!
And all who heard should see them there,
And all should cry, Beware! Beware!
His flashing eyes, his floating hair!
Weave a circle round him thrice,
And close your eyes with holy dread,
For he on honeydew hath fed,
And drunk the milk of Paradise.

FRAGMENT

Seaward, white gleaming thro' the busy scud
With arching Wings, the sea mew o'er my head
Posts on, as bent on speed, now passaging
Edges the stiffer Breeze, now, yielding, drifts,
Now floats upon the air, and sends from far
A wildly-wailing Note.

HEXAMETERS

William, my teacher, my friend! dear William and dear
    Dorothea!
Smooth out the folds of my letter, and place it on desk or
    on table;
Place it on table or desk; and your right hands loosely
    half-closing,
Gently sustain them in air, and extending the digit
    didactic,
Rest it a moment on each of the forks of the five-forkéd
    left hand,
Twice on the breadth of the thumb, and once on the
    tip of each finger;
Read with a nod of the head in a humoring recitativo;
And, as I live, you will see my hexameters hopping before
    you.
This is a galloping measure; a hop, and a trot, and a
    gallop!

All my hexameters fly, like stags pursued by the stag-
    hounds,
Breathless and panting, and ready to drop, yet flying still
    onwards,
I would full fain pull in my hard-mouthed runaway
    hunter;
But our English Spondeans are clumsy yet impotent
    curb-reins;
And so to make him go slowly, no way left have I but
    to lame him.

William, my head and my heart! dear Poet that feelest
    and thinkest!

Dorothy, eager of soul, my most affectionate sister!
Many a mile, O! many a wearisome mile are ye distant,
Long, long comfortless roads, with no one eye that doth
    know us.
O! it is all too far to send you mockeries idle:
Yea, and I feel it not right! But O! my friends, my
    belovéd!
Feverish and wakeful I lie—I am weary of feeling and
    thinking.
Every thought is worn *down*, I am weary yet cannot be
    vacant.
Five long hours have I tossed, rheumatic heats, dry and
    flushing,
Gnawing behind in my head, and wandering and
    throbbing about me,
Busy and tiresome, my friends, as the beat of the boding
    night-spider.

    I forget the beginning of the line:
    . . . my eyes are a burthen,
Now unwillingly closed, now open and aching with
    darkness.
O! what a life is the eye! what a strange and inscrutable
    essence!
Him that is utterly blind, nor glimpses the fire that
    warms him;
Him that never beheld the swelling breast of his
    mother;
Him that smiled in his gladness as a babe that smiles in
    its slumber;
Even for him it exists, it moves and stirs in its prison;
Lives with a separate life, and "Is it a Spirit?" he
    murmurs:
"Sure it has thoughts of its own, and to see is only a
    language."

*There was a great deal more, which I have forgotten.
. . . The last line which I wrote, I remember, and write
it for the truth of the sentiment, scarcely less true in
company than in pain and solitude —*

William, my head and my heart! dear William and dear
    Dorothea!
You have all in each other; but I am lonely, and want
    you!

THE HOMERIC HEXAMETER

DESCRIBED AND EXEMPLIFIED

Strongly it bears us along in swelling and limitless billows,
Nothing before and nothing behind but the sky and the
    ocean.

THE OVIDIAN ELEGIAC METER

DESCRIBED AND EXEMPLIFIED

In the hexameter rises the fountain's silvery column;
In the pentameter aye falling in melody back.

CATULLIAN HENDECASYLLABLES

Hear, my belovéd, an old Milesian story!—
High, and embosom'd in congregated laurels,
Glimmer'd a temple upon a breezy headland;
In the dim distance amid the skiey billows
Rose a fair island; the god of flocks had blest it.
From the far shores of the bleat-resounding island
Oft by the moonlight a little boat came floating,
Came to the sea cave beneath the breezy headland,
Where amid myrtles a pathway stole in mazes
Up to the groves of the high embosom'd temple.
There in a thicket of dedicated roses,
Oft did a priestess, as lovely as a vision,
Pouring her soul to the son of Cytherea,
Pray him to hover around the slight canoe-boat,
And with invisible pilotage to guide it
Over the dusk wave, until the nightly sailor
Shivering with ecstasy sank upon her bosom.

LINES

I stood on Brocken's sovran height, and saw
Woods crowding upon woods, hills over hills,
A surging scene, and only limited
By the blue distance. Heavily my way
Downward I dragged through fir groves evermore,
Where bright green moss heaves in sepulchral forms
Speckled with sunshine; and, but seldom heard,
The sweet bird's song became a hollow sound;
And the breeze, murmuring indivisibly,
Preserved its solemn murmur most distinct
From many a note of many a waterfall,
And the brook's chatter; 'mid whose islet-stones
The dingy kidling with its tinkling bell
Leaped frolicsome, or old romantic goat
Sat, his white beard slow waving. I moved on
In low and languid mood: for I had found
That outward forms, the loftiest, still receive
Their finer influence from the Life within—
Fair cyphers else: fair, but of import vague
Or unconcerning, where the heart not finds
History or prophecy of friend, or child,
Or gentle maid, our first and early love,
Or father, or the venerable name
Of our adoréd country! O thou Queen,
Thou delegated Deity of Earth,
O dear, dear England! how my longing eye
Turned westward, shaping in the steady clouds
Thy sands and high white cliffs!

                        My native Land!
Filled with the thought of thee this heart was proud,
Yea, mine eye swam with tears: that all the view
From sovran Brocken, woods and woody hills,
Floated away, like a departing dream,
Feeble and dim! Stranger, these impulses
Blame thou not lightly; nor will I profane,
With hasty judgment or injurious doubt,
That man's sublimer spirit, who can feel
That God is everywhere! the God who framed
Mankind to be one mighty family,
Himself our Father, and the World our Home.

LINES COMPOSED IN A
CONCERT ROOM

Nor cold, nor stern, my soul! yet I detest
   These scented Rooms, where, to a gaudy throng,
Heaves the proud Harlot her distended breast,
   In intricacies of laborious song.

These feel not Music's genuine power, nor deign
   To melt at Nature's passion-warbled plaint;
But when the long-breathed singer's uptrilled strain
   Bursts in a squall—they gape for wonderment.

Hark! the deep buzz of Vanity and Hate!
   Scornful, yet envious, with self-torturing sneer
My lady eyes some maid of humbler state,
   While the pert Captain, or the primmer Priest,
   Prattles accordant scandal in her ear.

O give me, from this heartless scene released,
   To hear our old Musician, blind and gray
(Whom stretching from my nurse's arms I kissed),
   His Scottish tunes and warlike marches play,
By moonshine, on the balmy summer night,
   The while I dance amid the tedded hay
With merry maids, whose ringlets toss in light.

Or lies the purple evening on the bay
Of the calm glossy lake, O let me hide
   Unheard, unseen, behind the alder trees,
For round their roots the fisher's boat is tied,
   On whose trim seat doth Edmund stretch at ease,
And while the lazy boat sways to and fro,

Breathes in his flute sad airs, so wild and slow,
That his own cheek is wet with quiet tears.

But O, dear Anne! when midnight wind careers,
And the gust pelting on the outhouse shed
   Makes the cock shrilly in the rainstorm crow,
   To hear thee sing some ballad full of woe,
Ballad of shipwreck'd sailor floating dead,
   Whom his own true love buried in the sands!
Thee, gentle woman, for thy voice remeasures
Whatever tones and melancholy pleasures
   The things of Nature utter; birds or trees,
Or moan of ocean gale in weedy caves,
Or where the stiff grass mid the heath-plant waves,
   Murmur and music thin of sudden breeze.

LOVE

All thoughts, all passions, all delights,
Whatever stirs this mortal frame,
All are but ministers of Love,
    And feed his sacred flame.

Oft in my waking dreams do I
Live o'er again that happy hour,
When midway on the mount I lay,
    Beside the ruined tower.

The moonshine, stealing o'er the scene
Had blended with the lights of eve;
And she was there, my hope, my joy,
    My own dear Genevieve!

She leant against the arméd man,
The statue of the arméd knight;
She stood and listened to my lay,
    Amid the lingering light.

Few sorrows hath she of her own,
My hope! my joy! my Genevieve!
She loves me best, whene'er I sing
    The songs that make her grieve.

I played a soft and doleful air,
I sang an old and moving story—
An old rude song, that suited well
    That ruin wild and hoary.

She listened with a flitting blush,
With downcast eyes and modest grace;

For well she knew, I could not choose
        But gaze upon her face.

I told her of the Knight that wore
Upon his shield a burning brand;
And that for ten long years he wooed
        The Lady of the Land.

I told her how he pined: and ah!
The deep, the low, the pleading tone
With which I sang another's love,
        Interpreted my own.

She listened with a flitting blush,
With downcast eyes, and modest grace;
And she forgave me, that I gazed
        Too fondly on her face!

But when I told the cruel scorn
That crazed that bold and lovely Knight,
And that he crossed the mountain woods,
        Nor rested day nor night;

That sometimes from the savage den,
And sometimes from the darksome shade,
And sometimes starting up at once
        In green and sunny glade—

There came and looked him in the face
An angel beautiful and bright;
And that he knew it was a Fiend,
        This miserable Knight!

And that unknowing what he did,
He leaped amid a murderous band,
And saved from outrage worse than death
        The Lady of the Land!

And how she wept, and clasped his knees;
And how she tended him in vain—
And ever strove to expiate
    The scorn that crazed his brain—

And that she nursed him in a cave;
And how his madness went away,
When on the yellow forest leaves
    A dying man he lay—

His dying words—but when I reached
That tenderest strain of all the ditty,
My faltering voice and pausing harp
    Disturbed her soul with pity!

All impulses of soul and sense
Had thrilled my guileless Genevieve;
The music and the doleful tale,
    The rich and balmy eve;

And hopes, and fears that kindle hope,
An undistinguishable throng,
And gentle wishes long subdued,
    Subdued and cherished long!

She wept with pity and delight,
She blushed with love, and virgin-shame;
And like the murmur of a dream,
    I heard her breathe my name.

Her bosom heaved—she stepped aside,
As conscious of my look she stepped—
Then suddenly, with timorous eye
    She fled to me and wept.

She half-enclosed me with her arms,
She pressed me with a meek embrace;

And bending back her head, looked up,
    And gazed upon my face.

'Twas partly love, and partly fear,
And partly 'twas a bashful art,
That I might rather feel, than see,
    The swelling of her heart.

I calmed her fears, and she was calm,
And told her love with virgin pride;
And so I won my Genevieve,
    My bright and beauteous Bride.

DEJECTION: AN ODE

[WRITTEN APRIL 4, 1802]

Late, late yestreen I saw the new Moon,
With the old Moon in her arms;
And I fear, I fear, my Master dear!
We shall have a deadly storm.

Ballad of Sir Patrick Spence.

I

Well! If the Bard was weather-wise, who made
  The grand old ballad of Sir Patrick Spence,
  This night, so tranquil now, will not go hence
Unroused by winds, that ply a busier trade
Than those which mold yon cloud in lazy flakes,
Or the dull sobbing draft, that moans and rakes
Upon the strings of this Aeolian lute,
    Which better far were mute.
  For lo! the New Moon winter-bright!
  And overspread with phantom light,
  (With swimming phantom light o'erspread
  But rimmed and circled by a silver thread)
I see the old Moon in her lap, foretelling
  The coming-on of rain and squally blast.
And oh! that even now the gust were swelling,
  And the slant night-shower driving loud and fast!
Those sounds which oft have raised me, whilst they
    awed,
    And sent my soul abroad,
Might now perhaps their wonted impulse give,
Might startle this dull pain, and make it move and
    live!

II

A grief without a pang, void, dark, and drear,
　　A stifled, drowsy, unimpassioned grief,
　　Which finds no natural outlet, no relief,
　　　　In word, or sigh, or tear—
O Lady! fix this wan and heartless mood,
To other thoughts by yonder throstle woo'd,
　　All this long eve, so balmy and serene,
Have I been gazing on the western sky,
　　And its peculiar tint of yellow green:
And still I gaze—and with how blank an eye!
And those thin clouds above, in flakes and bars,
That give away their motion to the stars;
Those stars, that glide behind them or between,
Now sparkling, now bedimmed, but always seen:
Yon crescent Moon, as fixed as if it grew
In its own cloudless, starless lake of blue;
I see them all so excellently fair,
I see, not feel, how beautiful they are!

III

　　My genial spirits fail;
　　And what can these avail
To lift the smothering weight from off my breast?
　　It were a vain endeavor,
　　Though I should gaze forever
On that green light that lingers in the west:
I may not hope from outward forms to win
The passion and the life, whose fountains are within.

IV

O Lady! we receive but what we give,
And in our life alone does Nature live:
Ours is her wedding garment, ours her shroud!
　　And would we aught behold, of higher worth,
Than that inanimate cold world allowed

To the poor loveless ever-anxious crowd,
    Ah! from the soul itself must issue forth
A light, a glory, a fair luminous cloud
        Enveloping the Earth—
And from the soul itself must there be sent
    A sweet and potent voice, of its own birth,
Of all sweet sounds the life and element!

V

O pure of heart! thou need'st not ask of me
What this strong music in the soul may be!
What, and wherein it doth exist,
This light, this glory, this fair luminous mist,
This beautiful and beauty-making power.
    Joy, virtuous Lady! Joy that ne'er was given,
Save to the pure, and in their purest hour,
Life, and Life's effluence, cloud at once and shower,
Joy, Lady! is the spirit and the power,
Which wedding Nature to us gives in dower
    A new Earth and new Heaven,
Undreamt of by the sensual and the proud—
Joy is the sweet voice, Joy the luminous cloud—
        We in ourselves rejoice!
And thence flows all that charms or ear or sight,
    All melodies the echoes of that voice,
All colors a suffusion from that light.

VI

There was a time when, though my path was rough,
    This joy within me dallied with distress,
And all misfortunes were but as the stuff
    Whence Fancy made me dreams of happiness:
For hope grew round me, like the twining vine,
And fruits, and foliage, not my own, seemed mine.
But now afflictions bow me down to earth:
Nor care I that they rob me of my mirth;

But oh! each visitation
Suspends what nature gave me at my birth,
   My shaping spirit of Imagination.
For not to think of what I needs must feel,
   But to be still and patient, all I can;
And haply by abstruse research to steal
   From my own nature all the natural man—
   This was my sole resource, my only plan:
Till that which suits a part infects the whole,
And now is almost grown the habit of my soul.

VII

Hence, viper thoughts, that coil around my mind,
   Reality's dark dream!
I turn from you, and listen to the wind,
   Which long has raved unnoticed. What a scream
Of agony by torture lengthened out
That lute sent forth! Thou Wind, that rav'st without,
   Bare crag, or mountain tairn, or blasted tree,
Or pine grove whither woodman never clomb,
Or lonely house, long held the witches' home,
   Methinks were fitter instruments for thee,
Mad Lutanist! who in this month of showers,
Of dark-brown gardens, and of peeping flowers,
Mak'st Devils' yule, with worse than wintry song,
The blossoms, buds, and timorous leaves among.
   Thou Actor, perfect in all tragic sounds!
Thou mighty Poet, e'en to frenzy bold!
     What tell'st thou now about?
     'Tis of the rushing of an host in rout,
With groans, of trampled men, with smarting
       wounds—
At once they groan with pain, and shudder with the
       cold!
But hush! there is a pause of deepest silence!
   And all that noise, as of a rushing crowd,

With groans, and tremulous shudderings—all is over—
　　It tells another tale, with sounds less deep and loud!
　　　　A tale of less affright,
　　　　And tempered with delight,
As Otway's self had framed the tender lay—
　　　　'Tis of a little child
　　　　Upon a lonesome wild,
Not far from home, but she hath lost her way:
And now moans low in bitter grief and fear,
And now screams loud, and hopes to make her mother
　　　　hear.

VIII

'Tis midnight, but small thoughts have I of sleep:
Full seldom may my friend such vigils keep!
Visit her, gentle Sleep! with wings of healing,
　　And may this storm be but a mountain-birth,
May all the stars hang bright above her dwelling,
　　Silent as though they watched the sleeping Earth!
　　　　With light heart may she rise,
　　　　Gay fancy, cheerful eyes,
　　Joy lift her spirit, joy attune her voice;
To her may all things live, from pole to pole,
Their life the eddying of her living soul!
　　O simple spirit, guided from above,
Dear Lady! friend devoutest of my choice,
Thus mayest thou ever, evermore rejoice.

THE PICTURE

OR, THE LOVER'S RESOLUTION

Through weeds and thorns, and matted underwood
I force my way; now climb, and now descend
O'er rocks, or bare or mossy, with wild foot
Crushing the purple whorts; while oft unseen,
Hurrying along the drifted forest leaves,
The scared snake rustles. Onward still I toil,
I know not, ask not whither! A new joy,
Lovely as light, sudden as summer gust,
And gladsome as the firstborn of the spring,
Beckons me on, or follows from behind,
Playmate, or guide! The master-passion quelled,
I feel that I am free. With dun-red bark
The fir trees, and the unfrequent slender oak,
Forth from this tangle wild of bush and brake
Soar up, and form a melancholy vault
High o'er me, murmuring like a distant sea.

Here Wisdom might resort, and here Remorse;
Here too the lovelorn man, who, sick in soul,
And of this busy human heart aweary,
Worships the spirit of unconscious life
In tree or wildflower—Gentle lunatic!
If so he might not wholly cease to be,
He would far rather not be that he is;
But would be something that he knows not of,
In winds or waters, or among the rocks!

But hence, fond wretch! breathe not contagion here!
No myrtle walks are these: these are no groves
Where Love dare loiter! If in sullen mood

He should stray hither, the low stumps shall gore
His dainty feet, the briar and the thorn
Make his plumes haggard. Like a wounded bird
Easily caught, ensnare him, O ye Nymphs,
Ye Oreads chaste, ye dusky Dryades;
And you, ye Earth-winds! you that make at morn
The dewdrops quiver on the spiders' webs!
You, O ye wingless Airs! that creep between
The rigid stems of heath and bitten furze,
Within whose scanty shade, at summer noon,
The mother-sheep hath worn a hollow bed—
Ye, that now cool her fleece with dropless damp,
Now pant and murmur with her feeding lamb.
Chase, chase him, all ye Fays, and elfin Gnomes!
With prickles sharper than his darts bemock
His little Godship, making him perforce
Creep through a thornbush on yon hedgehog's
      back.

  This is my hour of triumph! I can now
With my own fancies play the merry fool,
And laugh away worse folly, being free.
Here will I seat myself, beside this old,
Hollow, and weedy oak, which ivy-twine
Clothes as with network: here will I couch my limbs,
Close by this river, in this silent shade,
As safe and sacred from the step of man
As an invisible world—unheard, unseen,
And listening only to the pebbly brook
That murmurs with a dead, yet tinkling sound;
Or to the bees, that in the neighboring trunk
Make honey-hoards. The breeze, that visits me,
Was never Love's accomplice, never raised
The tendril ringlets from the maiden's brow,
And the blue, delicate veins above her cheek;
Ne'er played the wanton—never half-disclosed

The maiden's snowy bosom, scattering thence
Eye-poisons for some love-distempered youth,
Who ne'er henceforth may see an aspen grove
Shiver in sunshine, but his feeble heart
Shall flow away like a dissolving thing.

Sweet breeze! thou only, if I guess aright,
Liftest the feathers of the robin's breast,
That swells its little breast, so full of song,
Singing above me, on the mountain ash.
And thou too, desert stream! no pool of thine,
Though clear as lake in latest summer eve,
Did e'er reflect the stately virgin's robe,
The face, the form divine, the downcast look
Contemplative! Behold! her open palm
Presses her cheek and brow! her elbow rests
On the bare branch of half-uprooted tree,
That leans towards its mirror! Who erewhile
Had from her countenance turned, or looked by
        stealth,
(For Fear is true-love's cruel nurse), he now
With steadfast gaze and unoffending eye,
Worships the watery idol, dreaming hopes
Delicious to the soul, but fleeting, vain,
E'en as that phantom world on which he gazed,
But not unheeded gazed: for see, ah! see,
The sportive tyrant with her left hand plucks
The heads of tall flowers that behind her grow,
Lychnis, and willow herb, and foxglove bells:
And suddenly, as one that toys with time,
Scatters them on the pool! Then all the charm
Is broken—all that phantom world so fair
Vanishes, and a thousand circlets spread,
And each misshape the other. Stay awhile,
Poor youth, who scarcely dar'st lift up thine eyes!
The stream will soon renew its smoothness, soon

The visions will return! And lo! he stays:
And soon the fragments dim of lovely forms
Come trembling back, unite, and now once more
The pool becomes a mirror; and behold
Each wildflower on the marge inverted there,
And there the half-uprooted tree—but where,
O where the virgin's snowy arm, that leaned
On its bare branch? He turns, and she is gone!
Homeward she steals through many a woodland
      maze
Which he shall seek in vain. Ill-fated youth!
Go, day by day, and waste thy manly prime
In mad love-yearning by the vacant brook,
Till sickly thoughts bewitch thine eyes, and thou
Behold'st her shadow still abiding there,
The Naiad of the mirror!
                Not to thee,
O wild and desert stream! belongs this tale:
Gloomy and dark art thou—the crowded firs
Spire from thy shores, and stretch across thy bed,
Making thee doleful as a cavern well:
Save when the shy kingfishers build their nest
On thy steep banks, no loves hast thou, wild stream!

   This be my chosen haunt—emancipate
From Passion's dreams, a freeman, and alone,
I rise and trace its devious course. O lead,
Lead me to deeper shades and lonelier glooms.
Lo! stealing through the canopy of firs,
How fair the sunshine spots that mossy rock,
Isle of the river, whose disparted waves
Dart off asunder with an angry sound,
How soon to reunite! And see! they meet,
Each in the other lost and found: and see
Placeless, as spirits, one soft water-sun
Throbbing within them, heart at once and eye!

With its soft neighborhood of filmy clouds,
The stains and shadings of forgotten tears,
Dimness o'erswum with luster! Such the hour
Of deep enjoyment, following love's brief feuds
And hark, the noise of a near waterfall!
I pass forth into light—I find myself
Beneath a weeping birch (most beautiful
Of forest trees, the Lady of the Woods),
Hard by the brink of a tall weedy rock
That overbrows the cataract. How bursts
The landscape on my sight! Two crescent hills
Fold in behind each other, and so make
A circular vale, and landlocked, as might seem,
With brook and bridge, and gray stone cottages,
Half-hid by rocks and fruit trees. At my feet,
The whortle berries are bedewed with spray,
Dashed upwards by the furious waterfall.
How solemnly the pendent ivy mass
Swings in its winnow: All the air is calm.
The smoke from cottage chimneys, tinged with light,
Rises in columns; from this house alone,
Close by the waterfall, the column slants,
And feels its ceaseless breeze. But what is this?
That cottage, with its slanting chimney smoke,
And close beside its porch a sleeping child,
His dear head pillowed on a sleeping dog—
One arm between its forelegs, and the hand
Holds loosely its small handful of wildflowers
Unfilletted, and of unequal lengths.
A curious picture, with a master's haste
Sketched on a strip of pinky-silver skin,
Peeled from the birchen bark! Divinest maid!
Yon bark her canvas, and those purple berries
Her pencil! See, the juice is scarcely dried
On the fine skin! She has been newly here;
And lo! yon patch of heath has been her couch—

The pressure still remains! O blesséd couch!
For this may'st thou flower early, and the sun,
Slanting at eve, rest bright, and linger long
Upon thy purple bells! O Isabel!
Daughter of genius! stateliest of our maids!
More beautiful than whom Alcaeus wooed,
The Lesbian woman of immortal song!
O child of genius! stately, beautiful,
And full of love to all, save only me,
And not ungentle e'en to me! My heart,
Why beats it thus? Through yonder coppice wood
Needs must the pathway turn, that leads straightway
On to her father's house. She is alone!
The night draws on—such ways are hard to hit—
And fit it is I should restore this sketch,
Dropt unawares, no doubt. Why should I yearn
To keep the relique? 'twill but idly feed
The passion that consumes me. Let me haste!
The picture in my hand which she has left;
She cannot blame me that I followed her:
And I may be her guide the long wood through.

INSCRIPTION FOR A FOUNTAIN
ON A HEATH

This Sycamore, oft musical with bees—
Such tents the Patriarchs loved! O long unharmed
May all its agéd boughs o'er-canopy
The small round basin, which this jutting stone
Keeps pure from falling leaves! Long may the Spring,
Quietly as a sleeping infant's breath,
Send up cold waters to the traveler
With soft and even pulse! Nor ever cease
Yon tiny cone of sand its soundless dance,
Which at the bottom, like a Fairy's Page,
As merry and no taller, dances still,
Nor wrinkles the smooth surface of the Fount.
Here Twilight is and Coolness: here is moss,
A soft seat, and a deep and ample shade.
Thou may'st toil far and find no second tree.
Drink, Pilgrim, here; here rest! and if thy heart
Be innocent, here too shalt thou refresh
Thy spirit, listening to some gentle sound,
Or passing gale or hum of murmuring bees!

A DAYDREAM

My eyes make pictures, when they are shut:
    I see a fountain, large and fair,
A willow and a ruined hut,
    And thee, and me and Mary there.
O Mary! make thy gentle lap our pillow!
Bend o'er us, like a bower, my beautiful green willow!

    A wild-rose roofs the ruined shed,
        And that and summer well agree:
    And lo! where Mary leans her head,
        Two dear names carved upon the tree!
And Mary's tears, they are not tears of sorrow:
Our sister and our friend will both be here tomorrow.

    'Twas day! but now few, large, and bright,
        The stars are round the crescent moon!
    And now it is a dark warm night,
        The balmiest of the month of June!
A glowworm fall'n, and on the marge remounting
Shines, and its shadow shines, fit stars for our sweet
        fountain.

    O ever—ever be thou blest!
        For dearly, Asra! love I thee!
    This brooding warmth across my breast,
        This depth of tranquil bliss—ah, me!
Fount, tree and shed are gone, I know not whither,
But in one quiet room we three are still together.

    The shadows dance upon the wall,
        By the still dancing fire flames made;

And now they slumber, moveless all!
　　And now they melt to one deep shade!
But not from me shall this mild darkness steal thee:
I dream thee with mine eyes, and at my heart I feel
　　　　thee!

　　Thine eyelash on my cheek doth play—
　　　　'Tis Mary's hand upon my brow!
　　But let me check this tender lay
　　　　Which none may hear but she and thou!
Like the still hive at quiet midnight humming,
Murmur it to yourselves, ye two beloved women!

ANSWER TO A CHILD'S QUESTION

Do you ask what the birds say? The Sparrow, the Dove,
The Linnet and Thrush say, "I love and I love!"
In the winter they're silent—the wind is so strong;
What it says, I don't know, but it sings a loud song.
But green leaves, and blossoms, and sunny warm
　　weather,
And singing, and loving—all come back together.
But the Lark is so brimful of gladness and love,
The green fields below him, the blue sky above,
That he sings, and he sings; and forever sings he—
"I love my Love, and my Love loves me!"

THE PAINS OF SLEEP

Ere on my bed my limbs I lay,
It hath not been my use to pray
With moving lips or bended knees;
But silently, by slow degrees,
My spirit I to Love compose,
In humble trust mine eyelids close,
With reverential resignation,
No wish conceived, no thought exprest,
Only a sense of supplication;
A sense o'er all my soul imprest
That I am weak, yet not unblest,
Since in me, round me, everywhere
Eternal Strength and Wisdom are.

But yesternight I prayed aloud
In anguish and in agony,
Up-starting from the fiendish crowd
Of shapes and thoughts that tortured me:
A lurid light, a trampling throng,
Sense of intolerable wrong,
And whom I scorned, those only strong!
Thirst of revenge, the powerless will
Still baffled, and yet burning still!
Desire with loathing strangely mixed
On wild or hateful objects fixed.
Fantastic passions! maddening brawl!
And shame and terror over all!
Deeds to be hid which were not hid,
Which all confused I could not know
Whether I suffered, or I did:
For all seemed guilt, remorse or woe,

My own or others' still the same
Life-stifling fear, soul-stifling shame.

So two nights passed: the night's dismay
Saddened and stunned the coming day.
Sleep, the wide blessing, seemed to me
Distemper's worst calamity.
The third night, when my own loud scream
Had waked me from the fiendish dream,
O'ercome with sufferings strange and wild,
I wept as I had been a child;
And having thus by tears subdued
My anguish to a milder mood,
Such punishments, I said, were due
To natures deepliest stained with sin—
For aye entempesting anew
The unfathomable hell within,
The horror of their deeds to view,
To know and loathe, yet wish and do!
Such griefs with such men well agree,
But wherefore, wherefore fall on me?
To be beloved is all I need,
And whom I love, I love indeed.

EPITAPH

Here sleeps at length poor Col. and without screaming,
Who died, as he had always lived, a-dreaming;
Shot dead, while sleeping, by the Gout within,
Alone, and all unknown, at E'nbro' in an Inn.

THE EXCHANGE

We pledged our hearts, my love and I—
   I in my arms the maiden clasping;
I could not guess the reason why,
   But, oh! I trembled like an aspen.

Her father's love she bade me gain;
   I went, but shook like any reed!
I strove to act the man—in vain!
   We had exchanged our hearts indeed.

PHANTOM

All look and likeness caught from earth
All accident of kin and birth,
Had pass'd away. There was no trace
Of aught on that illumined face,
Uprais'd beneath the rifted stone
But of one spirit all her own—
She, she herself, and only she,
Shone through her body visibly.

A SUNSET

Upon the mountain's edge with light touch resting,
There a brief while the globe of splendor sits
   And seems a creature of the earth; but soon
      More changeful than the Moon,
To wane fantastic his great orb submits,
Or cone or mow of fire: till sinking slowly
Even to a star at length he lessens wholly.

Abrupt, as Spirits vanish, he is sunk!
   A soul-like breeze possesses all the wood.
The boughs, the sprays have stood
As motionless as stands the ancient trunk!
But every leaf through all the forest flutters,
And deep the cavern of the fountain mutters.

WHAT IS LIFE?

   Resembles life what once was deem'd of light,
   Too ample in itself for human sight?
An absolute self—an element ungrounded—
All that we see, all colors of all shade
      By encroach of darkness made?—
Is very life by consciousness unbounded?
And all the thoughts, pains, joys of mortal breath,
A war-embrace of wrestling life and death?

THE BLOSSOMING OF THE
SOLITARY DATE TREE

A LAMENT

I

Beneath the blaze of a tropical sun the mountain peaks are the Thrones of Frost, through the absence of objects to reflect the rays. "What no one with us shares, seems scarce our own." The presence of a ONE,

The best belov'd, who loveth me the best,

is for the heart, what the supporting air from within is for the hollow globe with its suspended car. Deprive it of this, and all without, that would have buoyed it aloft even to the seat of the gods, becomes a burthen and crushes it into flatness.

II

The finer the sense for the beautiful and the lovely, and the fairer and lovelier the object presented to the sense; the more exquisite the individual's capacity of joy, and the more ample his means and opportunities of enjoyment, the more heavily will he feel the ache of solitariness, the more unsubstantial becomes the feast spread around him. What matters it, whether in fact the viands and the ministering graces are shadowy or real, to him who has not hand to grasp nor arms to embrace them?

III

Imagination; honorable aims;
Free commune with the choir that cannot die;

Science and song; delight in little things,
The buoyant child surviving in the man;
Fields, forests, ancient mountains, ocean, sky,
With all their voices—O dare I accuse
My earthly lot as guilty of my spleen,
Or call my destiny niggard! O no! no!
It is her largeness, and her overflow,
Which being incomplete, disquieteth me so!

IV

For never touch of gladness stirs my heart,
But tim'rously beginning to rejoice
Like a blind Arab, that from sleep doth start
In lonesome tent, I listen for thy voice.
Belovéd! 'tis not thine; thou art not there!
Then melts the bubble into idle air,
And wishing without hope I restlessly despair.

V

The mother with anticipated glee
Smiles o'er the child, that, standing by her chair
And flatt'ning its round cheek upon her knee,
Looks up, and doth its rosy lips prepare
To mock the coming sounds. At that sweet sight
She hears her own voice with a new delight;
And if the babe perchance should lisp the notes aright,

VI

Then is she tenfold gladder than before!
But should disease or chance the darling take,
What then avail those songs, which sweet of yore
Were only sweet for their sweet echo's sake?
Dear maid! no prattler at a mother's knee
Was e'er so dearly prized as I prize thee:
Why was I made for Love and Love denied to me?

TO WILLIAM WORDSWORTH

COMPOSED ON THE NIGHT AFTER HIS RECITATION OF A POEM ON THE GROWTH OF AN INDIVIDUAL MIND

Friend of the wise! and Teacher of the Good!
Into my heart have I received that Lay
More than historic, that prophetic Lay
Wherein (high theme by thee first sung aright)
Of the foundations and the building up
Of a Human Spirit thou hast dared to tell
What may be told, to the understanding mind
Revealable; and what within the mind
By vital breathings secret as the soul
Of vernal growth, oft quickens in the heart
Thoughts all too deep for words!—

                                 Theme hard as high!
Of smiles spontaneous, and mysterious fears
(The firstborn they of Reason and twin-birth),
Of tides obedient to external force,
And currents self-determined, as might seem,
Or by some inner Power; of moments awful,
Now in thy inner life, and now abroad,
When power streamed from thee, and thy soul received
The light reflected, as a light bestowed—
Of fancies fair, and milder hours of youth,
Hyblean murmurs of poetic thought
Industrious in its joy, in vales and glens
Native or outland, lakes and famous hills!
Or on the lonely highroad, when the stars
Were rising; or by secret mountain streams,
The guides and the companions of thy way!

Of more than Fancy, of the Social Sense
Distending wide, and man beloved as man,
Where France in all her towns lay vibrating
Like some becalméd bark beneath the burst
Of Heaven's immediate thunder, when no cloud
Is visible, or shadow on the main.
For thou wert there, thine own brows garlanded,
Amid the tremor of a realm aglow,
Amid a mighty nation jubilant,
When from the general heart of human kind
Hope sprang forth like a full-born Deity!
——Of that dear Hope afflicted and struck down,
So summoned homeward, thenceforth calm and sure
From the dread watchtower of man's absolute self,
With light unwaning on her eyes, to look
Far on—herself a glory to behold,
The Angel of the vision! Then (last strain)
Of Duty, chosen Laws controlling choice,
Action and joy!—An Orphic song indeed,
A song divine of high and passionate thoughts
To their own music chaunted!

                              O great Bard!
Ere yet that last strain dying awed the air,
With steadfast eye I viewed thee in the choir
Of ever-enduring men. The truly great
Have all one age, and from one visible space
Shed influence! They, both in power and act,
Are permanent, and Time is not with them,
Save as it worketh for them, they in it.
Nor less a sacred Roll, than those of old,
And to be placed, as they, with gradual fame
Among the archives of mankind, thy work
Makes audible a linkéd lay of Truth,
Of Truth profound a sweet continuous lay,
Not learnt, but native, her own natural notes!
Ah! as I listened with a heart forlorn,

The pulses of my being beat anew:
And even as Life returns upon the drowned,
Life's joy rekindling roused a throng of pains—
Keen pangs of Love, awakening as a babe
Turbulent, with an outcry in the heart;
And fears self-willed, that shunned the eye of Hope;
And Hope that scarce would know itself from Fear;
Sense of past Youth, and Manhood come in vain,
And Genius given, and knowledge won in vain;
And all which I had culled in wood-walks wild,
And all which patient toil had reared, and all,
Commune with thee had opened out—but flowers
Strewed on my corse, and borne upon my bier
In the same coffin, for the selfsame grave!

That way no more! and ill beseems it me,
Who came a welcomer in herald's guise,
Singing of Glory, and Futurity,
To wander back on such unhealthful road,
Plucking the poisons of self-harm! And ill
Such intertwine beseems triumphal wreaths
Strew'd before thy advancing!

                      Nor do thou,
Sage Bard! impair the memory of that hour
Of thy communion with my nobler mind
By pity or grief, already felt too long!
Nor let my words import more blame than needs.
The tumult rose and ceased: for Peace is nigh
Where Wisdom's voice has found a listening heart.
Amid the howl of more than wintry storms,
The Halcyon hears the voice of vernal hours
Already on the wing.

                Eve following eve,
Dear tranquil time, when the sweet sense of Home
Is sweetest! moments for their own sake hailed

And more desired, more precious, for thy song,
In silence listening, like a devout child,
My soul lay passive, by thy various strain
Driven as in surges now beneath the stars,
With momentary stars of my own birth,
Fair constellated foam, still darting off
Into the darkness; now a tranquil sea,
Outspread and bright, yet swelling to the moon.

And when—O Friend! my comforter and guide!
Strong in thyself, and powerful to give strength!—
Thy long sustainéd Song finally closed,
And thy deep voice had ceased—yet thou thyself
Wert still before my eyes, and round us both
That happy vision of belovéd faces—
Scarce conscious, and yet conscious of its close
I sate, my being blended in one thought
(Thought was it? or aspiration? or resolve?)
Absorbed, yet hanging still upon the sound—
And when I rose, I found myself in prayer.

AN ANGEL VISITANT

Within these circling hollies woodbine-clad—
Beneath this small blue roof of vernal sky—
How warm, how still! Tho' tears should dim mine eye,
Yet will my heart for days continue glad,
For here, my love, thou art, and here am I!

RECOLLECTIONS OF LOVE

I

How warm this woodland wild Recess!
　Love surely hath been breathing here;
　And this sweet bed of heath, my dear!
Swells up, then sinks with faint caress,
　As if to have you yet more near.

II

Eight springs have flown, since last I lay
　On seaward Quantock's heathy hills,
　Where quiet sounds from hidden rills
Float here and there, like things astray,
　And high o'er head the skylark shrills.

III

No voice as yet had made the air
　Be music with your name, yet why
　That asking look? that yearning sigh?
That sense of promise everywhere?
　Belovéd! flew your spirit by?

IV

As when a mother doth explore
　The rose-mark on her long-lost child,
　I met, I loved you, maiden mild!
As whom I long had loved before—
　So deeply had I been beguiled.

V

You stood before me like a thought,
　A dream remembered in a dream.

But when those meek eyes first did seem
To tell me, Love within you wrought—
O Greta, dear domestic stream!

VI

Has not, since then, Love's prompture deep,
    Has not Love's whisper evermore
    Been ceaseless, as thy gentle roar?
Sole voice, when other voices sleep,
    Dear under-song in clamor's hour.

[ITS OWN DELIGHT]

And in Life's noisiest hour
There whispers still the ceaseless love of thee,
The heart's self-solace⎫ and soliloquy.
        commune ⎭

You mold my Hopes you fashion me within:
    And to the leading love-throb in the heart,
    Through all my being, through my pulses beat;
You lie in all my many thoughts like Light,
    Like the fair light of Dawn, or summer Eve,
    On rippling stream, or cloud-reflecting lake;
And looking to the Heaven that bends above you,
How oft! I bless the lot that made me love you.
    And my heart mantles in its own delight.

TO TWO SISTERS

[MARY MORGAN AND CHARLOTTE BRENT]

A WANDERER'S FAREWELL

To know, to esteem, to love—and then to part—
Makes up life's tale to many a feeling heart;
Alas for some abiding-place of love,
O'er which my spirit, like the mother dove,
Might brood with warming wings!
                              O fair! O kind!
Sisters in blood, yet each with each intwined
More close by sisterhood of heart and mind!
Me disinherited in form and face
By nature, and mishap of outward grace;
Who, soul and body, through one guiltless fault
Waste daily with the poison of sad thought,
Me did you soothe, when solace hoped I none!
And as on unthaw'd ice the winter sun,
Though stern the frost, though brief the genial day,
You bless my heart with many a cheerful ray;
For gratitude suspends the heart's despair,
Reflecting bright though cold your image there.
Nay more! its music by some sweeter strain
Makes us live o'er our happiest hours again,
Hope reappearing dim in memory's guise—
Even thus did you call up before mine eyes
Two dear, dear Sisters, prized all price above,
Sisters, like you, with more than sister's love;
So like you *they*, and so in *you* were seen
Their relative statures, tempers, looks, and mien,
That oft, dear ladies! you have been to me
At once a vision and reality.

Sight seem'd a sort of memory, and amaze
Mingled a trouble with affection's gaze.

Oft to my eager soul I whisper blame,
A Stranger bid it feel the Stranger's shame—
My eager soul, impatient of the name,
No strangeness owns, no Stranger's form descries:
The chidden heart spreads trembling on the eyes.

First-seen I gazed, as I would look you thro'!
My best-beloved regain'd their youth in you—
And still I ask, though now familiar grown,
Are you for *their* sakes dear, or for your own?
O doubly dear! may Quiet with you dwell!

In Grief I love you, yet I love you well!
Hope long is dead to me! an orphan's tear
Love wept despairing o'er his nurse's bier.
Yet still she flutters o'er her grave's green slope:
For Love's despair is but the ghost of Hope!

Sweet Sisters! were you placed around one hearth
With those, your other selves in shape and worth,
Far rather would I sit in solitude,
Fond recollections all my fond heart's food,
And dream of *you*, sweet Sisters! (ah! not mine!)
And only *dream* of you (ah! dream and pine!)
Than boast the presence and partake the pride,
And shine in the eye, of all the world beside.

A TOMBLESS EPITAPH

'Tis true, Idoloclastes Satyrane!
(So call him, for so mingling blame with praise,
And smiles with anxious looks, his earliest friends,
Masking his birth-name, wont to character
His wild-wood fancy and impetuous zeal),
'Tis true that, passionate for ancient truths,
And honoring with religious love the Great
Of elder times, he hated to excess,
With an unquiet and intolerant scorn,
The hollow puppets of a hollow Age,
Ever idolatrous, and changing ever
Its worthless Idols! Learning, Power, and Time,
(Too much of all) thus wasting in vain war
Of fervid colloquy. Sickness, 'tis true,
Whole years of weary days, besieged him close,
Even to the gates and inlets of his life!
But it is true, no less, that strenuous, firm,
And with a natural gladness, he maintained
The citadel unconquered, and in joy
Was strong to follow the delightful Muse.
For not a hidden path, that to the shades
Of the beloved Parnassian forest leads,
Lurked undiscovered by him; not a rill
There issues from the fount of Hippocrene,
But he had traced it upward to its source,
Through open glade, dark glen, and secret dell,
Knew the gay wildflowers on its banks, and culled
Its med'cinable herbs. Yea, oft alone,
Piercing the long-neglected holy cave,
The haunt obscure of old Philosophy,
He bade with lifted torch its starry walls

Sparkle, as erst they sparkled to the flame
Of odorous lamps tended by Saint and Sage.
O framed for calmer times and nobler hearts!
O studious Poet, eloquent for truth!
Philosopher! contemning wealth and death,
Yet docile, childlike, full of Life and Love!
Here, rather than on monumental stone,
This record of thy worth thy Friend inscribes,
Thoughtful, with quiet tears upon his cheek.

PSYCHE

The butterfly the ancient Grecians made
The soul's fair emblem, and its only name—
But of the soul, escaped the slavish trade
Of mortal life!—For in this earthly frame
Ours is the reptile's lot, much toil, much blame,
Manifold motions making little speed,
And to deform and kill the things whereon we feed.

THE VISIONARY HOPE

Sad lot, to have no Hope! Though lowly kneeling
He fain would frame a prayer within his breast,
Would fain entreat for some sweet breath of healing,
That his sick body might have ease and rest;
He strove in vain! the dull sighs from his chest
Against his will the stifling load revealing,
Though Nature forced; though like some captive guest,
Some royal prisoner at his conqueror's feast,
An alien's restless mood but half-concealing,
The sternness on his gentle brow confessed,
Sickness within and miserable feeling:
Though obscure pangs made curses of his dreams,
And dreaded sleep, each night repelled in vain,
Each night was scattered by its own loud screams:
Yet never could his heart command, though fain,
One deep full wish to be no more in pain.

That Hope, which was his inward bliss and boast,
Which waned and died, yet ever near him stood,
Though changed in nature, wander where he would—
For Love's Despair is but Hope's pining Ghost!
For this one hope he makes his hourly moan,
He wishes and can wish for this alone!
Pierced, as with light from Heaven, before its gleams
(So the love-stricken visionary deems)
Disease would vanish, like a summer shower,
Whose dews fling sunshine from the noon-tide bower!
Or let it stay! yet this one Hope should give
Such strength that he would bless his pains and live.

TIME, REAL AND IMAGINARY

AN ALLEGORY

On the wide level of a mountain's head,
(I knew not where, but 'twas some fairy place)
Their pinions, ostrich-like, for sails outspread,
Two lovely children run an endless race,
     A sister and a brother!
     This far outstripp'd the other;
  Yet ever runs she with reverted face,
  And looks and listens for the boy behind:
     For he, alas! is blind!
O'er rough and smooth with even step he passed,
And knows not whether he be first or last.

FOR A MARKET-CLOCK

(IMPROMPTU)

What now, O Man! thou dost or mean'st to do
Will help to give thee peace, or make thee rue,
When hovering o'er the Dot this hand shall tell
The moment that secures thee Heaven or Hell!

AN INVOCATION

From REMORSE

[ACT III, SCENE I, LINES 69–82.]

Hear, sweet Spirit, hear the spell,
Lest a blacker charm compel!
So shall the midnight breezes swell
With thy deep long-lingering knell.

And at evening evermore,
In a chapel on the shore,
Shall the chaunter, sad and saintly,
Yellow tapers burning faintly,
Doleful masses chaunt for thee,
        Miserere Domine!

Hush! the cadence dies away
    On the quiet moonlight sea:
The boatmen rest their oars and say,
        Miserere Domine!

HUMAN LIFE

ON THE DENIAL OF IMMORTALITY

If dead, we cease to be; if total gloom
   Swallow up life's brief flash for aye, we fare
As summer gusts, of sudden birth and doom,
   Whose sound and motion not alone declare,
But are their whole of being! If the breath
   Be Life itself, and not its task and tent,
If even a soul like Milton's can know death;
   O Man! thou vessel purposeless, unmeant,
Yet drone-hive strange of phantom purposes!
   Surplus of Nature's dread activity,
Which, as she gazed on some nigh-finished vase,
Retreating slow, with meditative pause,
   She formed with restless hands unconsciously.
Blank accident! nothing's anomaly!
   If rootless thus, thus substanceless thy state,
Go, weigh thy dreams, and be thy hopes, thy fears,
The counterweights!—Thy laughter and thy tears
   Mean but themselves, each fittest to create
And to repay the other! Why rejoices
   Thy heart with hollow joy for hollow good?
   Why cowl thy face beneath the mourner's hood?
Why waste thy sighs, and thy lamenting voices,
   Image of Image, Ghost of Ghostly Elf,
That such a thing as thou feel'st warm or cold?
Yet what and whence thy gain, if thou withhold
   These costless shadows of thy shadowy self?
Be sad! be glad! be neither! seek, or shun!
Thou hast no reason why! Thou canst have none;
Thy being's being is contradiction.

SONG

From ZAPOLYA

A sunny shaft did I behold,
   From sky to earth it slanted:
And poised therein a bird so bold—
   Sweet bird, thou wert enchanted!

He sank, he rose, he twinkled, he trolled
   Within that shaft of sunny mist;
His eyes of fire, his beak of gold,
   All else of amethyst!

And thus he sang: "Adieu! adieu!
Love's dreams prove seldom true.
The blossoms they make no delay:
The sparkling dew-drops will not stay.
   Sweet month of May,
      We must away;
         Far, far away!
           Today! today!"

HUNTING SONG

From ZAPOLYA

Up, up! ye dames, and lasses gay!
To the meadows trip away.
'Tis you must tend the flocks this morn,
And scare the small birds from the corn.
    Not a soul at home may stay:
        For the shepherds must go
        With lance and bow
    To hunt the wolf in the woods today.

Leave the hearth and leave the house
To the cricket and the mouse:
Find grannam out a sunny seat,
With babe and lambkin at her feet.
    Not a soul at home may stay:

        For the shepherds must go
        With lance and bow
    To hunt the wolf in the woods today.

TO NATURE

It may indeed be fantasy, when I
   Essay to draw from all created things
   Deep, heartfelt, inward joy that closely clings;
And trace in leaves and flowers that round me lie
Lessons of love and earnest piety.
   So let it be; and if the wide world rings
   In mock of this belief, it brings
Nor fear, nor grief, nor vain perplexity.
So will I build my altar in the fields,
   And the blue sky my fretted dome shall be,
And the sweet fragrance that the wildflower yields
   Shall be the incense I will yield to Thee,
Thee only God! and thou shalt not despise
Even me, the priest of this poor sacrifice.

FRAGMENT

The body,
Eternal Shadow of the finite Soul,
The Soul's self-symbol, its image of itself.
Its own yet not itself.

LIMBO

The sole true Something—This! In Limbo's Den
It frightens Ghosts, as here Ghosts frighten men.
Thence cross'd unseiz'd—and shall some fated hour
Be pulveriz'd by Demogorgon's power,
And given as poison to annihilate souls—
Even now it shrinks them—they shrink in as Moles
(Nature's mute monks, live mandrakes of the ground)
Creep back from Light—then listen for its sound—
See but to dread, and dread they know not why—
The natural alien of their negative eye.

'Tis a strange place, this Limbo!—not a Place,
Yet name it so—where Time and weary Space
Fettered from flight, with nightmare sense of fleeing,
Strive for their last crepuscular half-being—
Lank Space, and scytheless Time with branny hands
Barren and soundless as the measuring sands,
Not mark'd by flit of Shades—unmeaning they
As moonlight on the dial of the day!
But that is lovely—looks like Human Time,
An Old Man with a steady look sublime,
That stops his earthly task to watch the skies;
But he is blind—a Statue hath such eyes—
Yet having moonward turn'd his face by chance,
Gazes the orb with moon-like countenance,
With scant white hairs, with foretop bald and high,
He gazes still—his eyeless face all eye—
As 'twere an organ full of silent sight,
His whole face seemeth to rejoice in light!
Lip touching lip, all moveless, bust and limb—
He seems to gaze at that which seems to gaze on
        him!

No such sweet sights doth Limbo den immure,
Wall'd round, and made a spirit-jail secure,
By the mere horror of blank Naught-at-all,
Whose circumambience doth these ghosts enthrall.
A lurid thought is growthless, dull Privation,
Yet that is but a Purgatory curse;
Hell knows a fear far worse,
A fear—a future state—'tis positive Negation!

THE KNIGHT'S TOMB

Where is the grave of Sir Arthur O'Kellyn?
Where may the grave of that good man be?—
By the side of a spring, on the breast of Helvellyn,
Under the twigs of a young birch tree!
The oak that in summer was sweet to hear,
And rustled its leaves in the fall of the year,
And whistled and roared in the winter alone,
Is gone—and the birch in its stead is grown—
The Knight's bones are dust,
And his good sword rust—
His soul is with the saints, I trust.

NE PLUS ULTRA

Sole Positive of Night!
Antipathist of Light!
Fate's only essence! primal scorpion rod—
The one permitted opposite of God!—
Condenséd blackness and abysmal storm
Compacted to one scepter
Arms the Grasp enorm—
The Intercepter—
The Substance that still casts the shadow Death!—
The Dragon foul and fell—
The unrevealable,
And hidden one, whose breath
Gives wind and fuel to the fires of Hell!
Ah! sole despair
Of both th' eternities in Heaven!
Sole interdict of all-bedewing prayer,
The all-compassionate!
Save to the Lampads Seven
Reveal'd to none of all th' Angelic State,
Save to the Lampads Seven,
That watch the throne of Heaven!

ON DONNE'S POETRY

With Donne, whose muse on dromedary trots,
Wreathe iron pokers into true-love knots;
Rhyme's sturdy cripple, fancy's maze and clue,
Wit's forge and fire-blast, meaning's press and screw.

YOUTH AND AGE

Verse, a breeze mid blossoms straying,
Where Hope clung feeding, like a bee—
Both were mine! Life went a-maying
       With Nature, Hope, and Poesy,
           When I was young!

When I was young?—Ah, woeful When!
Ah! for the change 'twixt Now and Then!
This breathing house not built with hands,
This body that does me grievous wrong,
O'er aery cliffs and glittering sands,
How lightly then it flashed along—
Like those trim skiffs, unknown of yore,
On winding lakes and rivers wide,
That ask no aid of sail or oar,
That fear no spite of wind or tide!
Naught cared this body for wind or weather
When Youth and I lived in't together.

Flowers are lovely; Love is flower-like;
Friendship is a sheltering tree;
O! the joys, that came down shower-like,
Of Friendship, Love, and Liberty,
           Ere I was old!

Ere I was old? Ah woeful Ere,
Which tells me, Youth's no longer here!
O Youth! for years so many and sweet,
'Tis known, that Thou and I were one,
I'll think it but a fond conceit—
It cannot be that Thou art gone!

Thy vesper-bell hath not yet toll'd—
And thou wert aye a masker bold!
What strange disguise hast now put on,
To make believe, that thou art gone?
I see these locks in silvery slips,
This drooping gait, this altered size:
But Spring-tide blossoms on thy lips,
And tears take sunshine from thine eyes!
Life is but thought; so think I will
That Youth and I are housemates still.

Dew-drops are the gems of morning,
But the tears of mournful eve!
Where no hope is, life's a warning
That only serves to make us grieve,
                              When we are old:

That only serves to make us grieve
With oft and tedious taking-leave,
Like some poor nigh-related guest,
That may not rudely be dismist;
Yet hath outstay'd his welcome while,
And tells the jest without the smile.

FIRST ADVENT OF LOVE

O fair is Love's first hope to gentle mind!
As Eve's first star thro' fleecy cloudlet peeping;
And sweeter than the gentle southwest wind.
O'er willowy meads, and shadow'd waters creeping,
And Ceres' golden fields—the sultry hind
Meets it with brow uplift, and stays his reaping.

WORK WITHOUT HOPE

LINES COMPOSED FEBRUARY 21, 1825

All Nature seems at work. Slugs leave their lair—
The bees are stirring—birds are on the wing—
And Winter slumbering in the open air,
Wears on his smiling face a dream of Spring!
And I the while, the sole unbusy thing,
Nor honey make, nor pair, nor build, nor sing.

Yet well I ken the banks where amaranths blow,
Have traced the fount whence streams of nectar flow.
Bloom, O ye amaranths! bloom for whom ye may,
For me ye bloom not! Glide, rich streams, away!
With lips unbrightened, wreathless brow, I stroll:
And would you learn the spells that drowse my soul?
Work without Hope draws nectar in a sieve,
And Hope without an object cannot live.

SONG

Though veiled in spires of myrtle-wreath,
Love is a sword which cuts its sheath,
And through the clefts itself has made,
We spy the flashes of the blade!
But through the clefts itself has made
We likewise see Love's flashing blade,
By rust consumed, or snapt in twain;
And only hilt and stump remain.

A CHARACTER

A bird, who for his other sins
Had liv'd amongst the Jacobins;
Though like a kitten amid rats,
Or callow tit in nest of bats,
He much abhorr'd all democrats;
Yet nathless stood in ill report
Of wishing ill to Church and Court,
Tho' he'd nor claw, nor tooth, nor sting,
And learnt to pipe God save the King;
Tho' each day did new feathers bring,
All swore he had a leathern wing;
Nor polish'd wing, nor feather'd tail,
Nor down-clad thigh would aught avail;
And tho'—his tongue devoid of gall—
He civilly assur'd them all—
"A bird am I of Phoebus' breed,
And on the sunflower cling and feed;
My name, good Sirs, is Thomas Tit!"
The bats would hail him Brother Cit,
Or, at the furthest, cousin-german.
At length the matter to determine,
He publicly denounced the vermin;
He spared the mouse, he praised the owl;
But bats were neither flesh nor fowl.
Blood-sucker, vampire, harpy, ghoul,
Came in full clatter from his throat,
Till his old nest-mates chang'd their note
To hireling, traitor, and turncoat—
A base apostate who had sold
His very teeth and claws for gold—
And then his feathers!—sharp the jest—
No doubt he feather'd well his nest!

"A Tit indeed! aye, tit for tat—
With place and title, brother Bat,
We soon shall see how well he'll play
Count Goldfinch, or Sir Joseph Jay!"
    Alas, poor Bird! and ill-bestarr'd—
Or rather let us say, poor Bard!
And henceforth quit the allegoric,
With metaphor and simile,
For simple facts and style historic—
Alas, poor Bard! no gold had he;
Behind another's team he stept,
And plough'd and sow'd, while others reapt;
The work was his, but theirs the glory,
Sic vos non vobis, his whole story.
Besides, whate'er he wrote or said
Came from his heart as well as head;
And though he never left in lurch
His king, his country, or his church,
'Twas but to humor his own cynical
Contempt of doctrines Jacobinical;
To his own conscience only hearty,
'Twas but by chance he serv'd the party—
The selfsame things had said and writ,
Had Pitt been Fox, and Fox been Pitt;
Content his own applause to win,
Would never dash thro' thick and thin,
And he can make, so say the wise,
No claim who makes no sacrifice—
And bard still less—what claim had he,
Who swore it vex'd his soul to see
So grand a cause, so proud a realm,
With Goose and Goody at the helm;
Who long ago had fall'n asunder
But for their rivals' baser blunder,
The coward whine and Frenchified
Slaver and slang of the other side?—

Thus, his own whim his only bribe,
Our Bard pursued his old A.B.C.
Contented if he could subscribe
In fullest sense his name Ἔστησε;
('Tis Punic Greek for "he hath stood!")
Whate'er the men, the cause was good;
And therefore with a right good will,
Poor fool, he fights their battles still.
Tush! squeak'd the Bats—a mere bravado
To whitewash that base renegado;
'Tis plain unless you're blind or mad,
His conscience for the bays he barters—
And true it is—as true as sad—
These circlets of green baize he had—
But then, alas! they were his garters!
  Ah! silly Bard, unfed, untended,
His lamp but glimmer'd in its socket;
He lived unhonor'd and unfriended
With scarce a penny in his pocket—
Nay—tho' he hid it from the many—
With scarce a pocket for his penny!

CONSTANCY TO AN IDEAL OBJECT

Since all that beat about in Nature's range,
Or veer or vanish; why should'st thou remain
The only constant in a world of change,
O yearning Thought! that liv'st but in the brain?
Call to the Hours, that in the distance play,
The fairy people of the future day——
Fond Thought! not one of all that shining swarm
Will breathe on thee with life-enkindling breath,
Till when, like strangers shelt'ring from a storm,
Hope and Despair meet in the porch of Death!
Yet still thou haunt'st me; and though well I see,
She is not thou, and only thou art she,
Still, still as though some dear embodied Good,
Some living Love before my eyes there stood
With answering look a ready ear to lend,
I mourn to thee and say—"Ah! loveliest friend!
That this the meed of all my toils might be,
To have a home, an English home, and thee!"
Vain repetition! Home and Thou are one.
The peacefull'st cot, the moon shall shine upon,
Lulled by the thrush and wakened by the lark,
Without thee were but a becalméd bark,
Whose Helmsman on an ocean waste and wide
Sits mute and pale his moldering helm beside.

And art thou nothing? Such thou art, as when
The woodman winding westward up the glen
At wintry dawn, where o'er the sheep-track's maze
The viewless snow-mist weaves a glist'ning haze,
Sees full before him, gliding without tread,
An image with a glory round its head;
The enamored rustic worships its fair hues,
Nor knows he makes the shadow, he pursues!

PHANTOM OR FACT

A DIALOGUE IN VERSE

AUTHOR

A lovely form there sate beside my bed,
And such a feeding calm its presence shed,
A tender love so pure from earthly leaven,
That I unnethe the fancy might control,
'Twas my own spirit newly come from heaven,
Wooing its gentle way into my soul!
But ah! the change—It had not stirr'd, and yet—
Alas! that change how fain would I forget!
That shrinking back, like one that had mistook!
That weary, wandering, disavowing look!
'Twas all another, feature, look, and frame,
And still, methought, I knew, it was the same!

FRIEND

This riddling tale, to what does it belong?
Is't history? vision? or an idle song?
Or rather say at once, within what space
Of time this wild disastrous change took place?

AUTHOR

Call it a moment's work (and such it seems)
This tale's a fragment from the life of dreams;
But say, that years matur'd the silent strife,
And 'tis a record from the dream of life.

REASON

["Finally, what is Reason? You have often asked me:
and this is my answer"—]

Whene'er the mist, that stands 'twixt God and thee,
Defecates to a pure transparency,
That intercepts no light and adds no stain—
There Reason is, and then begins her reign!

But alas!
——"tu stesso, ti fai grosso
Col falso immaginar, si che non vedi
Ciò che vedresti, se l'avessi scosso."
DANTE, *Paradiso*, CANTO I.

SELF-KNOWLEDGE
—*E coelo descendit* γνῶθι σεαυτόν—Juvenal, xi, 27

Γνῶθι σεαυτόν—and is this the prime
And heaven-sprung adage of the olden time!—
Say, canst thou make thyself?—Learn first that trade—
Haply thou mayst know what thyself had made.
What hast thou, Man, that thou dar'st call thine
    own?—
What is there in thee, Man, that can be known—
Dark fluxion, all unfixable by thought,
A phantom dim of past and future wrought,
Vain sister of the worm—life, death, soul, clod—
Ignore thyself, and strive to know thy God!

EPITAPH

Stop, Christian passerby!—Stop, child of God,
And read with gentle breast. Beneath this sod
A poet lies, or that which once seem'd he.
O, lift one thought in prayer for S.T.C.;
That he who many a year with toil of breath
Found death in life, may here find life in death!
Mercy for praise—to be forgiven for fame
He ask'd, and hoped, through Christ. Do thou the same!

The Rime of the
Ancient Mariner

THE RIME OF THE ANCIENT MARINER

IN SEVEN PARTS

Facile credo, plures esse Naturas invisibiles quam visibiles in rerum universitate. Sed horum omnium familiam quis nobis enarrabit? et gradus et cognationes et discrimina et singulorum munera? Quid agunt? quae loca habitant? Harum rerum notitiam semper ambivit ingenium humanum, nunquam attigit. Juvat, interea, non diffiteor, quandoque in animo, tanquam in tabulâ, majoris et melioris mundi imaginem contemplari: ne mens assuefacta hodiernae vitae minutiis se contrahat nimis, et tota subsidat in pusillas cogitationes. Sed veritati interea invigilandum est, modusque servandus, ut certa ab incertis, diem a nocte, distinguamus.—

T. BURNET, *Archaeol. Phil.* p. 68.

ARGUMENT

How a Ship having passed the Line was driven by storms to the cold Country towards the South Pole; and how from thence she made her course to the tropical Latitude of the Great Pacific Ocean; and of the strange things that befell; and in what manner the Ancyent Marinere came back to his own Country.

PART I

An ancient Mariner meeteth three Gallants bidden to a wedding-feast, and detaineth one.

It is an ancient Mariner,
And he stoppeth one of three.
"By thy long gray beard and glittering eye,
Now wherefore stoppst thou me?

The Bridegrooms doors are opened wide,
And I am next of kin;
The guests are met, the feast is set:
May'st hear the merry din."

He holds him with his skinny hand,
"There was a ship," quoth he.
"Hold off! unhand me, gray-beard loon!"
Eftsoons his hand dropt he.

The Wedding-
Guest is spell-
bound by the eye
of the old seafar-
ing man, and con-
strained to hear
his tale.

He holds him with his glittering eye—
The Wedding-Guest stood still,
And listens like a three-years' child:
The Mariner hath his will.

The Wedding-Guest sat on a stone:
He cannot choose but hear;
And thus spake on that ancient man,
The bright-eyed Mariner.

"The ship was cheered, the harbor cleared,
Merrily did we drop
Below the kirk, below the hill,
Below the lighthouse top.

The Mariner tells
how the ship
sailed southward
with a good wind
and fair weather
till it reached the
Line.

The Sun came up upon the left,
Out of the sea came he!
And he shone bright, and on the right
Went down into the sea.

Higher and higher every day,
Till over the mast at noon—"
The Wedding-Guest here beat his breast,
For he heard the loud bassoon.

The Wedding-
Guest heareth the
bridal music; but
the Mariner con-
tinueth his tale.

The bride hath paced into the hall,
Red as a rose is she;
Nodding their heads before her goes
The merry minstrelsy.

The Wedding-Guest he beat his breast,
Yet he cannot choose but hear;

And thus spake on that ancient man,
The bright-eyed Mariner.

The Ship driven
by a storm toward
the south pole.
"And now the STORM-BLAST came, and he
Was tyrannous and strong;
He struck with his o'ertaking wings,
And chased us south along.

With sloping masts and dipping prow,
As who pursued with yell and blow
Still treads the shadow of his foe,
And forward bends his head,
The ship drove fast, loud roared the blast,
And southward aye we fled.

And now there came both mist and snow,
And it grew wondrous cold:
And ice, mast-high, came floating by,
As green as emerald.

The land of ice,
and of fearful
sounds where no
living thing was to
be seen.
And through the drifts the snowy clifts
Did send a dismal sheen:
Nor shapes of men nor beasts we ken—
The ice was all between.

The ice was here, the ice was there,
The ice was all around:
It cracked and growled, and roared and howled,
Like noises in a swound!

Till a great sea-
bird, called the
Albatross, came
through the snow-
fog, and was
received with
great joy and hos-
pitality.
At length did cross an Albatross,
Thorough the fog it came;
As if it had been a Christian soul,
We hailed it in God's name.

It ate the food it ne'er had eat,
And round and round it flew.

The ice did split with a thunder-fit;
The helmsman steered us through!

And a good south wind sprung up behind;
The Albatross did follow,
And every day, for food or play,
Came to the mariners' hollo!

In mist or cloud, on mast or shroud,
It perched for vespers nine;
Whiles all the night, through fog-smoke white,
Glimmered the white Moonshine."

"God save thee, ancient Mariner!
From the fiends, that plague thee thus!—
Why look'st thou so?"—With my crossbow
I shot the ALBATROSS.

PART II

The Sun now rose upon the right:
Out of the sea came he,
Still hid in mist, and on the left
Went down into the sea.

And the good south wind still blew behind,
But no sweet bird did follow,
Nor any day for food or play
Came to the mariners' hollo!

And I had done a hellish thing,
And it would work 'em woe:
For all averred, I had killed the bird
That made the breeze to blow.
Ah wretch! said they, the bird to slay,
That made the breeze to blow!

But when the fog
cleared off, they
justify the same,
and thus make
themselves
accomplices in the
crime.

Nor dim nor red, like Gods own head,
The glorious Sun uprist:
Then all averred, I had killed the bird
That brought the fog and mist.
'Twas right, said they, such birds to slay,
That bring the fog and mist.

The fair breeze
continues; the
ship enters the
Pacific Ocean,
and sails north-
ward, even till it
reaches the Line.

The fair breeze blew, the white foam flew,
The furrow followed free;
We were the first that ever burst
Into that silent sea.

The ship hath
been suddenly
becalmed.

Down dropt the breeze, the sails dropt down,
'Twas sad as sad could be;
And we did speak only to break
The silence of the sea!

All in a hot and copper sky,
The bloody Sun, at noon,
Right up above the mast did stand,
No bigger than the Moon.

Day after day, day after day,
We stuck, nor breath nor motion;
As idle as a painted ship
Upon a painted ocean.

And the Albatross
begins to be
avenged.

Water, water, everywhere,
And all the boards did shrink;
Water, water, everywhere,
Nor any drop to drink.

The very deep did rot: O Christ!
That ever this should be!
Yea, slimy things did crawl with legs
Upon the slimy sea.

About, about, in reel and rout
The death-fires danced at night;
The water, like a witch's oils,
Burnt green, and blue and white.

A Spirit had fol-
lowed them; one
of the invisible
inhabitants of this
planet, neither

And some in dreams assuréd were
Of the Spirit that plagued us so;
Nine fathom deep he had followed us
From the land of mist and snow.

departed souls nor angels; concerning whom the learned Jew, Josephus, and the
Platonic Constantinopolitan, Michael Psellus, may be consulted. They are very numerous, and there is no climate or element without one or more.

And every tongue, through utter drought,
Was withered at the root;
We could not speak, no more than if
We had been choked with soot.

The shipmates, in
their sore distress,
would fain throw
the whole guilt on
the ancient
Mariner: in sign

Ah! well a-day! what evil looks
Had I from old and young!
Instead of the cross, the Albatross
About my neck was hung.

whereof they hang the dead sea-bird round his neck.

PART III

There passed a weary time. Each throat
Was parched, and glazed each eye.
A weary time! a weary time!
How glazed each weary eye,
When looking westward, I beheld

The ancient
Mariner behold-
eth a sign in the
element afar off.

A something in the sky.

At first it seemed a little speck,
And then it seemed a mist;

It moved and moved, and took at last
A certain shape, I wist.

A speck, a mist, a shape, I wist!
And still it neared and neared:
As if it dodged a water-sprite,
It plunged and tacked and veered.

At its nearer approach, it seemeth him to be a ship; and at a dear ransom he freeth his speech from the bonds of thirst.

With throats unslaked, with black lips baked,
We could nor laugh nor wail;
Through utter drought all dumb we stood!
I bit my arm, I sucked the blood,
And cried, A sail! a sail!

With throats unslaked, with black lips baked,
Agape they heard me call:
A flash of joy;
Gramercy! they for joy did grin,
And all at once their breath drew in,
As they were drinking all.

And horror follows. For can it be a ship that comes onward without wind or tide?

See! See! (I cried) she tacks no more!
Hither to work us weal;
Without a breeze, without a tide,
She steadies with upright keel!

The western wave was all a-flame.
The day was well nigh done!
Almost upon the western wave
Rested the broad bright Sun;
When that strange shape drove suddenly
Betwixt us and the Sun.

It seemeth him but the skeleton of a ship.

And straight the Sun was flecked with bars,
(Heaven's Mother send us grace!)
As if through a dungeon grate he peered
With broad and burning face.

Alas! (thought I, and my heart beat loud)
How fast she nears and nears!
Are those *her* sails that glance in the Sun,
Like restless gossameres?

Are those *her* ribs through which the Sun
Did peer, as through a grate?
And is that Woman all her crew?
Is that a DEATH? and are there two?
Is DEATH that woman's mate?

Her lips were red, *her* looks were free,
Her locks were yellow as gold:
Her skin was as white as leprosy,
The Nightmare LIFE-IN-DEATH was she,
Who thicks man's blood with cold.

The naked hulk alongside came,
And the twain were casting dice;
"The game is done! I've won! I've won!"
Quoth she, and whistles thrice.

The Sun's rim dips; the stars rush out:
At one stride comes the dark;
With far-heard whisper, o'er the sea,
Off shot the specter-bark.

We listened and looked sideways up!
Fear at my heart, as at a cup,
My lifeblood seemed to sip!
The stars were dim, and thick the night,
The steersman's face by his lamp gleamed
    white;

From the sails the dew did drip—
Till clomb above the eastern bar
The hornéd Moon, with one bright star
Within the nether tip.

One after
another,

One after one, by the star-dogged Moon,
Too quick for groan or sigh,
Each turned his face with ghastly pang,
And cursed me with his eye.

His shipmates
drop down dead.

Four times fifty living men,
(And I heard nor sigh nor groan)
With heavy thump, a lifeless lump,
They dropped down one by one.

But Life-in-Death
begins her work
on the ancient
Mariner.

The souls did from their bodies fly—
They fled to bliss or woe!
And every soul, it passed me by,
Like the whizz of my crossbow!"

PART IV

The Wedding-
Guest feareth that
a Spirit is talking
to him;

"I fear thee, ancient Mariner!
I fear thy skinny hand!
And thou art long, and lank, and broken
As is the ribbed sea-sand.

I fear thee and thy glittering eye,
And thy skinny hand, so brown."—

But the ancient
Mariner assureth
him of his bodily
life, and pro-
ceedeth to relate
his horrible
penance.

"Fear not, fear not, thou Wedding-Guest!
This body dropt not down.

Alone, alone, all, all alone,
Alone on a wide wide sea!
And never a saint took pity on
My soul in agony.

He despiseth the
creatures of the
calm,

The many men, so beautiful!
And they all dead did lie:
And a thousand thousand slimy things
Lived on; and so did I.

And envieth that
they should live,
and so many lie
dead.

I looked upon the rotting sea,
And drew my eyes away;
I looked upon the rotting deck,
And there the dead men lay.

I looked to heaven, and tried to pray;
But or ever a prayer had gusht,
A wicked whisper came, and made
My heart as dry as dust.

I closed my lids, and kept them close,
And the balls like pulses beat;
For the sky and the sea, and the sea and
    the sky
Lay like a load on my weary eye,
And the dead were at my feet.

But the curse
liveth for him in
the eye of the
dead men.

The cold sweat melted from their limbs,
Nor rot nor reek did they:
The look with which they looked on me
Had never passed away.

An orphan's curse would drag to hell
A spirit from on high;
But oh! more horrible than that
Is the curse in a dead man's eye!
Seven days, seven nights, I saw that curse,
And yet I could not die.

In his loneliness
and fixedness he
yearneth towards
the journeying
Moon, and the
stars that still sojourn, yet still move onward; and everywhere the blue sky belongs to
them, and is their appointed rest, and their native country and their own natural
homes which they enter unannounced, as lords that are certainly expected and yet
there is a silent joy at their arrival.

The moving Moon went up the sky,
And nowhere did abide:
Softly she was going up,
And a star or two beside—

Her beams bemocked the sultry main,
Like April hoarfrost spread;
But where the ship's huge shadow lay,
The charméd water burnt alway
A still and awful red.

Beyond the shadow of the ship,
I watched the water snakes:
They moved in tracks of shining white,
And when they reared, the elfish light
Fell off in hoary flakes.

Within the shadow of the ship
I watched their rich attire:
Blue, glossy green, and velvet black,
They coiled and swam; and every track
Was a flash of golden fire.

O happy living things! no tongue
Their beauty might declare:
A spring of love gushed from my heart,

And I blessed them unaware:
Sure my kind saint took pity on me,
And I blessed them unaware.

The selfsame moment I could pray;
And from my neck so free
The Albatross fell off, and sank
Like lead into the sea.

PART V

Oh sleep! it is a gentle thing,
Beloved from pole to pole!
To Mary Queen the praise be given!
She sent the gentle sleep from Heaven,
That slid into my soul.

By grace of the
holy Mother, the
ancient Mariner is
refreshed with
rain.

The silly buckets on the deck,
That had so long remained,
I dreamt that they were filled with dew;
And when I awoke, it rained.

My lips were wet, my throat was cold,
My garments all were dank;
Sure I had drunken in my dreams,
And still my body drank.

I moved, and could not feel my limbs:
I was so light—almost
I thought that I had died in sleep,
And was a blessèd ghost.

He heareth
sounds and seeth
strange signs and
commotions in
the sky and the
element.

And soon I heard a roaring wind:
It did not come anear;
But with its sound it shook the sails,
That were so thin and sere.

The upper air burst into life!
And a hundred fire-flags sheen,
To and fro they were hurried about!
And to and fro, and in and out,
The wan stars danced between.

And the coming wind did roar more loud,
And the sails did sigh like sedge;
And the rain poured down from one black cloud;
The Moon was at its edge.

The thick black cloud was cleft, and still
The Moon was at its side:
Like waters shot from some high crag,
The lightning fell with never a jag,
A river steep and wide.

The loud wind never reached the ship,
Yet now the skip moved on!
Beneath the lightning and the Moon
The dead men gave a groan.

They groaned, they stirred, they all uprose,
Nor spake, nor moved their eyes;
It had been strange, even in a dream,
To have seen those dead men rise.

The helmsman steered, the ship moved on;
Yet never a breeze up-blew;
The mariners all 'gan work the ropes,
Where they were wont to do;
They raised their limbs like lifeless tools—
We were a ghastly crew.

The body of my brother's son
Stood by me, knee to knee:
The body and I pulled at one rope,
But he said naught to me."

"I fear thee, ancient Manner!"
"Be calm, thou Wedding-Guest!
'Twas not those souls that fled in pain,
Which to their corses came again,
But a troop of spirits blest:

For when it dawned—they dropped their arms,
And clustered round the mast;
Sweet sounds rose slowly through their
      mouths,
And from their bodies passed.

Around, around, flew each sweet sound,
Then darted to the Sun;

Slowly the sounds came back again,
Now mixed, now one by one.

Sometimes a-dropping from the sky
I heard the skylark sing;
Sometimes all little birds that are,
How they seemed to fill the sea and air
With their sweet jargoning!

And now 'twas like all instruments,
Now like a lonely flute;
And now it is an angel's song,
That makes the heavens be mute.

It ceased; yet still the sails made on
A pleasant noise till noon,
A noise like of a hidden brook
In the leafy month of June,
That to the sleeping woods all night
Singeth a quiet tune.

Till noon we quietly sailed on,
Yet never a breeze did breathe:
Slowly and smoothly went the ship,
Moved onward from beneath.

The lonesome
Spirit from the
south pole carries
on the ship as far
as the Line, in
obedience to the
angelic troop, but
still requireth
vengeance.

Under the keel nine fathom deep,
From the land of mist and snow,
The spirit slid: and it was he
That made the ship to go.
The sails at noon left off their tune,
And the ship stood still also.

The Sun, right up above the mast,
Had fixed her to the ocean:
But in a minute she 'gan stir,

With a short uneasy motion—
Backwards and forwards half her length
With a short uneasy motion.

Then like a pawing horse let go,
She made a sudden bound:
It flung the blood into my head,
And I fell down in a swound.

The Polar Spirit's
fellow-demons,
the invisible
inhabitants of the
element, take part
in his wrong; and
two of them
relate, one to the
other, that
penance long and
heavy for the
ancient Mariner
hath been accord-
ed to the Polar
Spirit, who retur-
neth southward.

How long in that same fit I lay,
I have not to declare;
But ere my living life returned,
I heard and in my soul discerned
Two voices in the air.

"Is it he?" quoth one, "Is this the man?
By him who died on cross,
With his cruel bow he laid full low
The harmless Albatross.

The spirit who bideth by himself
In the land of mist and snow,
He loved the bird that loved the man
Who shot him with his bow."

The other was a softer voice,
As soft as honeydew:
Quoth he, "The man hath penance done,
And penance more will do."

PART VI

FIRST VOICE

"But tell me, tell me! speak again,
Thy soft response renewing—

What makes that ship drive on so fast?
What is the ocean doing?"

SECOND VOICE

"Still as a slave before his lord,
The ocean hath no blast;
His great bright eye most silently
Up to the Moon is cast—

If he may know which way to go;
For she guides him smooth or grim.
See, brother, see! how graciously
She looketh down on him."

FIRST VOICE

The Mariner hath
been cast into a
trance; for the
angelic power
causeth the vessel
to drive north-
ward faster than
human life could
endure.

"But why drives on that ship so fast,
Without or wave or wind?"

SECOND VOICE

"The air is cut away before,
And closes from behind.

Fly, brother, fly! more high, more high!
Or we shall be belated:
For slow and slow that ship will go,
When the Mariner's trance is abated."

The supernatural
motion is retard-
ed; the Mariner
awakes, and his
penance begins
anew.

I woke, and we were sailing on
As in a gentle weather:
'Twas night, calm night, the moon was high;
The dead men stood together.

All stood together on the deck,
For a charnel-dungeon fitter:
All fixed on me their stony eyes,
That in the Moon did glitter.

The pang, the curse, with which they died,
Had never passed away:
I could not draw my eyes from theirs,
Nor turn them up to pray.

The curse is
finally expiated.
And now this spell was snapt: once more
I viewed the ocean green,
And looked far forth, yet little saw
Of what had else been seen—

Like one, that on a lonesome road
Doth walk in fear and dread,
And having once turned round walks on,
And turns no more his head;
Because he knows, a frightful fiend
Doth close behind him tread.

But soon there breathed a wind on me,
Nor sound nor motion made:
Its path was not upon the sea,
In ripple or in shade.

It raised my hair, it fanned my cheek
Like a meadow gale of spring—
It mingled strangely with my fears,
Yet it felt like a welcoming.

Swiftly, swiftly flew the ship,
Yet she sailed softly too:
Sweetly, sweetly blew the breeze—
On me alone it blew.

And the ancient
Mariner behold-
eth his native
country.
Oh! dream of joy! is this indeed
The lighthouse top I see?
Is this the hill? is this the kirk?
Is this mine own countree?

We drifted o'er the harbor bar,
And I with sobs did pray—
O let me be awake, my God!
Or let me sleep alway.

The harbor bay was clear as glass,
So smoothly it was strewn!
And on the bay the moonlight lay,
And the shadow of the Moon.

The rock shone bright, the kirk no less,
That stands above the rock:
The moonlight steeped in silentness
The steady weathercock.

And the bay was white with silent light,
Till rising from the same,
The angelic spirits leave the dead bodies, Full many shapes, that shadows were,
In crimson colors came.

And appear in their own forms of light. A little distance from the prow
Those crimson shadows were:
I turned my eyes upon the deck—
Oh, Christ! what saw I there!

Each corse lay flat, lifeless and flat,
And, by the holy rood!
A man all light, a seraph-man,
On every corse there stood.

This seraph-band, each waved his hand:
It was a heavenly sight!
They stood as signals to the land,
Each one a lovely light;

This seraph-band, each waved his hand,
No voice did they impart—

No voice; but oh! the silence sank
Like music on my heart.

But soon I heard the dash of oars,
I heard the Pilot's cheer;
My head was turned perforce away
And I saw a boat appear.

The Pilot and the Pilot's boy,
I heard them coming fast:
Dear Lord in Heaven! it was a joy
The dead men could not blast.

I saw a third—I heard his voice:
It is the Hermit good!
He singeth loud his godly hymns
That he makes in the wood.
He'll shrieve my soul, he'll wash away
The Albatross's blood.

PART VII

The Hermit of the Wood,

This Hermit good lives in that wood
Which slopes down to the sea.
How loudly his sweet voice he rears!
He loves to talk with marineres
That come from a far countree.

He kneels at morn, and noon, and eve—
He hath a cushion plump:
It is the moss that wholly hides
The rotted old oak stump.

The skiff-boat neared: I heard them talk,
"Why, this is strange, I trow!
Where are those lights so many and fair,
That signal made but now?"

"Strange, by my faith!" the Hermit said—
"And they answered not our cheer!
The planks looked warped! and see those
	sails,
How thin they are and sere!
I never saw aught like to them,
Unless perchance it were

Brown skeletons of leaves that lag
My forest brook along;
When the ivy-tod is heavy with snow,
And the owlet whoops to the wolf below,
That eats the she-wolfs young."

"Dear Lord! it hath a fiendish look—
(The Pilot made reply)
I am a-feared"—"Push on, push on!"
Said the Hermit cheerily.

The boat came closer to the ship,
But I nor spake nor stirred;
The boat came close beneath the ship,
And straight a sound was heard.

Under the water it rumbled on,
Still louder and more dread:
It reached the ship, it split the bay;
The skip went down like lead.

The ancient
Mariner is saved
in the Pilot's boat.
Stunned by that loud and dreadful sound,
Which sky and ocean smote,
Like one that hath been seven days drowned
My body lay afloat;
But swift as dreams, myself I found
Within the Pilot's boat:

Upon the whirl, where sank the skip,
The boat spun round and round;
And all was still, save that the hill
Was telling of the sound.

I moved my lips—the Pilot shrieked
And fell down in a fit;
The holy Hermit raised his eyes,
And prayed where he did sit.

I took the oars: the Pilot's boy,
Who now doth crazy go,
Laughed loud and long, and all the while
His eyes went to and fro.
"Ha! ha!" quoth he, "full plain I see,
The Devil knows how to row."

And now, all in my own countree,
I stood on the firm land!
The Hermit stepped forth from the boat,
And scarcely he could stand.

The ancient
Mariner earnestly
entreateth the
Hermit to shrieve
him; and the
penance of life
falls on him.

"O shrieve me, shrieve me, holy man!"
The Hermit crossed his brow.
"Say quick" quoth he, "I bid thee say—
What manner of man art thou?"

Forthwith this frame of mine was wrenched
With a woeful agony,
Which forced me to begin my tale;
And then it left me free.

And ever and
anon throughout
his future life an
agony con-
straineth him to
travel from land
to land;

Since then, at an uncertain hour,
That agony returns:
And till my ghastly tale is told,
This heart within me burns.

I pass, like night, from land to land;
I have strange power of speech;
That moment that his face I see,
I know the man that must hear me:
To him my tale I teach.

What loud uproar bursts from that door!
The wedding guests are there:
But in the garden bower the bride
And bridemaids singing are:
And hark the little vesper bell,
Which biddeth me to prayer!

O Wedding-Guest! this soul hath been
Alone on a wide wide sea:
So lonely 'twas, that God himself
Scarce seeméd there to be.

O sweeter than the marriage feast,
'Tis sweeter far to me,
To walk together to the kirk
With a goodly company!—

To walk together to the kirk,
And all together pray,
While each to his great Father bends,
Old men, and babes, and loving friends
And youths and maidens gay!

And to teach by his own example, love and reverence to all things that God made and loveth.

Farewell, farewell! but this I tell
To thee, thou Wedding-Guest!
He prayeth well, who loveth well
Both man and bird and beast.

He prayeth best, who loveth best
All things both great and small;

For the dear God who loveth us,
He made and loveth all."

The Mariner, whose eye is bright,
Whose beard with age is hoar,
Is gone: and now the Wedding-Guest
Turned from the bridegroom's door.

He went like one that hath been stunned,
And is of sense forlorn:
A sadder and a wiser man,
He rose the morrow morn.

Christabel

CHRISTABEL

The first part of the following poem was written in the year 1797, at Stowey, in the county of Somerset. The second part, after my return from Germany, in the year 1800, at Keswick, Cumberland. It is probable that if the poem had been finished at either of the former periods, or if even the first and second part had been published in the year 1800, the impression of its originality would have been much greater than I dare at present expect. But for this I have only my own indolence to blame. The dates are mentioned for the exclusive purpose of precluding charges of plagiarism or servile imitation from myself. For there is amongst us a set of critics, who seem to hold, that every possible thought and image is traditional; who have no notion that there are such things as fountains in the world, small as well as great; and who would therefore charitably derive every rill they behold flowing, from a perforation made in some other man's tank. I am confident, however, that as far as the present poem is concerned, the celebrated poets whose writings I might be suspected of having imitated, either in particular passages, or in the tone and the spirit of the whole, would be among the first to vindicate me from the charge, and, on any striking coincidence, would permit me to address them in this doggerel version of two monkish Latin hexameters.

> 'Tis mine and it is likewise yours;
> But an if this will not do;
> Let it be mine, good friend! for I
> Am the poorer of the two.

I have only to add that the meter of Christabel is not, properly speaking, irregular, though it may seem so from its being founded on a new principle: namely, that of counting in each line the accents, not the syllables. Though the latter may vary from seven to twelve, yet in each line the accents will be found to be only four. Nevertheless, this occasional variation in number of syllables is not introduced wantonly, or for the mere ends of convenience, but in correspondence with some transition in the nature of the imagery or passion.

PART I

'Tis the middle of night by the castle clock,
And the owls have awakened the crowing cock;
Tu—whit!——Tu—whoo!
And hark, again! the crowing cock,
How drowsily it crew.

Sir Leoline, the Baron rich,
Hath a toothless mastiff bitch;
From her kennel beneath the rock
She maketh answer to the clock,
Four for the quarters, and twelve for the hour;
Ever and aye, by shine and shower,
Sixteen short howls, not over loud;
Some say, she sees my lady's shroud.

Is the night chilly and dark?
The night is chilly, but not dark.
The thin gray cloud is spread on high,
It covers but not hides the sky.
The moon is behind, and at the full;
And yet she looks both small and dull.
The night is chill, the cloud is gray:
'Tis a month before the month of May,
And the Spring comes slowly up this way.

The lovely lady, Christabel,
Whom her father loves so well,
What makes her in the wood so late,

A furlong from the castle gate?
She had dreams all yesternight
Of her own betrothéd knight;
And she in the midnight wood will pray
For the weal of her lover that's far away.

She stole along, she nothing spoke,
The sighs she heaved were soft and low,
And naught was green upon the oak
But moss and rarest mistletoe:
She kneels beneath the huge oak tree,
And in silence prayeth she.

The lady sprang up suddenly,
The lovely lady, Christabel!
It moaned as near, as near can be,
But what it is she cannot tell—
On the other side it seems to be,
Of the huge, broad-breasted, old oak tree.

The night is chill; the forest bare;
Is it the wind that moaneth bleak?
There is not wind enough in the air
To move away the ringlet curl
From the lovely lady's cheek—
There is not wind enough to twirl
The one red leaf, the last of its clan,
That dances as often as dance it can,
Hanging so light, and hanging so high,
On the topmost twig that looks up at the sky.

Hush beating heart of Christabel!
Jesu, Maria, shield her well!
She folded her arms beneath her cloak,
And stole to the other side of the oak.
    What sees she there?

There she sees a damsel bright,
Drest in a silken robe of white,
That shadowy in the moonlight shone:
The neck that made that white robe wan,
Her stately neck, and arms were bare;
Her blue-veined feet unsandal'd were,
And wildly glittered here and there
The gems entangled in her hair.
I guess, 'twas frightful there to see
A lady so richly clad as she—
Beautiful exceedingly!

Mary mother, save me now!
(Said Christabel,) And who art thou?

The lady strange made answer meet,
And her voice was faint and sweet—
Have pity on my sore distress,
I scarce can speak for weariness:
Stretch forth thy hand, and have no fear!
Said Christabel, How camest thou here?
And the lady, whose voice was faint and sweet,
Did thus pursue her answer meet—

My sire is of a noble line,
And my name is Geraldine:
Five warriors seized me yestermorn,
Me, even me, a maid forlorn:
They choked my cries with force and fright,
And tied me on a palfrey white.
The palfrey was as fleet as wind,
And they rode furiously behind.
They spurred amain, their steeds were white:
And once we crossed the shade of night.
As sure as Heaven shall rescue me,
I have no thought what men they be;
Nor do I know how long it is

(For I have lain entranced I wis)
Since one, the tallest of the five,
Took me from the palfrey's back,
A weary woman, scarce alive.

Some muttered words his comrades spoke:
He placed me underneath this oak;
He swore they would return with haste;
Whither they went I cannot tell—
I thought I heard, some minutes past,
Sounds as of a castle bell.
Stretch forth thy hand (thus ended she),
And help a wretched maid to flee.

Then Christabel stretched forth her hand,
And comforted fair Geraldine:
O well, bright dame! may you command
The service of Sir Leoline;
And gladly our stout chivalry
Will he send forth and friends withal
To guide and guard you safe and free
Home to your noble father's hall.

She rose: and forth with steps they passed
That strove to be, and were not, fast.
Her gracious stars the lady blest,
And thus spake on sweet Christabel:
All our household are at rest,
The hall as silent as the cell;
Sir Leoline is weak in health,
And may not well awakened be,
But we will move as if in stealth,
And I beseech your courtesy,
This night, to share your couch with me.

They crossed the moat, and Christabel
Took the key that fitted well;

A little door she opened straight,
All in the middle of the gate;
The gate that was ironed within and without,
Where an army in battle array had marched out.
The lady sank, belike through pain,
And Christabel with might and main
Lifted her up, a weary weight,
Over the threshold of the gate:
Then the lady rose again,
And moved, as she were not in pain.

So free from danger, free from fear,
They crossed the court: right glad they were.
And Christabel devoutly cried
To the lady by her side,
Praise we the Virgin all divine
Who hath rescued thee from thy distress!
Alas, alas! said Geraldine,
I cannot speak for weariness.
So free from danger, free from fear,
They crossed the court: right glad they were.

Outside her kennel, the mastiff old
Lay fast asleep, in moonshine cold.
The mastiff old did not awake,
Yet she an angry moan did make!
And what can ail the mastiff bitch?
Never till now she uttered yell
Beneath the eye of Christabel.
Perhaps it is the owlet's scritch:
For what can ail the mastiff bitch?

They passed the hall, that echoes still,
Pass as lightly as you will!
The brands were flat, the brands were dying,
Amid their own white ashes lying;
But when the lady passed, there came
A tongue of light, a fit of flame;

And Christabel saw the lady's eye,
And nothing else saw she thereby,
Save the boss of the shield of Sir Leoline tall,
Which hung in a murky old niche in the wall.
O softly tread, said Christabel,
My father seldom sleepeth well.

Sweet Christabel her feet doth bare,
And jealous of the listening air
They steal their way from stair to stair,
Now in glimmer, and now in gloom,
And now they pass the Baron's room,
As still as death, with stifled breath!
And now have reached her chamber door;
And now doth Geraldine press down
The rushes of the chamber floor.

The moon shines dim in the open air,
And not a moonbeam enters here.
But they without its light can see
The chamber carved so curiously,
Carved with figures strange and sweet,
All made out of the carver's brain,
For a lady's chamber meet:
The lamp with twofold silver chain
Is fastened to an angel's feet.

The silver lamp burns dead and dim;
But Christabel the lamp will trim.
She trimmed the lamp, and made it bright,
And left it swinging to and fro,
While Geraldine, in wretched plight,
Sank down upon the floor below.

O weary lady, Geraldine,
I pray you, drink this cordial wine!
It is a wine of virtuous powers;
My mother made it of wildflowers.

And will your mother pity me,
Who am a maiden most forlorn?
Christabel answered—Woe is me!
She died the hour that I was born.
I have heard the gray-haired friar tell
How on her death-bed she did say,
That she should hear the castle bell
Strike twelve upon my wedding day.
O mother dear! that thou wert here!
I would, said Geraldine, she were!

But soon with altered voice, said she—
"Off, wandering mother! Peak and pine!
I have power to bid thee flee."
Alas! what ails poor Geraldine?
Why stares she with unsettled eye?
Can she the bodiless dead espy?
And why with hollow voice cries she,
"Off, woman, off! this hour is mine—
Though thou her guardian spirit be,
Off, woman, off! 'tis given to me."

Then Christabel knelt by the lady's side,
And raised to heaven her eyes so blue—
Alas! said she, this ghastly ride—
Dear lady! it hath wildered you!
The lady wiped her moist cold brow,
And faintly said, "'tis over now!"

Again the wildflower wine she drank:
Her fair large eyes 'gan glitter bright,
And from the floor whereon she sank,
The lofty lady stood upright:
She was most beautiful to see,
Like a lady of a far countrée.

And thus the lofty lady spake—
"All they who live in the upper sky.

Do love you, holy Christabel!
And you love them, and for their sake
And for the good which me befell,
Even I in my degree will try,
Fair maiden, to requite you well
But now unrobe yourself; for I
Must pray, ere yet in bed I lie."

Quoth Christabel, So let it be!
And as the lady bade, did she.
Her gentle limbs did she undress,
And lay down in her loveliness.

But through her brain of weal and woe
So many thoughts moved to and fro,
That vain it were her lids to close;
So half-way from the bed she rose,
And on her elbow did recline
To look at the lady Geraldine.

Beneath the lamp the lady bowed,
And slowly rolled her eyes around;
Then drawing in her breath aloud,
Like one that shuddered, she unbound
The cincture from beneath her breast:
Her silken robe, and inner vest,
Dropt to her feet, and full in view,
Behold! her bosom and half her side—
A sight to dream of, not to tell!
O shield her! shield sweet Christabel!

Yet Geraldine nor speaks nor stirs;
Ah! what a stricken look was hers!
Deep from within she seems half-way
To lift some weight with sick assay,
And eyes the maid and seeks delay;
Then suddenly, as one defied,
Collects herself in scorn and pride,

And lay down by the Maiden's side!—
And in her arms the maid she took,
      Ah wel-a-day!
And with low voice and doleful look
These words did say:
"In the touch of this bosom there worketh a spell,
Which is lord of thy utterance, Christabel!
Thou knowest tonight, and wilt know tomorrow,
This mark of my shame, this seal of my sorrow;
      But vainly thou warrest,
        For this is alone in
      Thy power to declare,
        That in the dim forest
      Thou heard'st a low moaning,
And found'st a bright lady, surpassingly fair;
And didst bring her home with thee in love and in
      charity,
To shield her and shelter her from the damp air."

THE CONCLUSION TO PART I

It was a lovely sight to see
The lady Christabel, when she
Was praying at the old oak tree.
      Amid the jaggéd shadows
      Of mossy leafless boughs,
      Kneeling in the moonlight,
      To make her gentle vows;
Her slender palms together prest,
Heaving sometimes on her breast;
Her face resigned to bliss or bale—
Her face, oh call it fair not pale,
And both blue eyes more bright than clear,
Each about to have a tear.

With open eyes (ah woe is me!)
Asleep, and dreaming fearfully,

Fearfully dreaming, yet, I wis,
Dreaming that alone, which is—
O sorrow and shame! Can this be she,
The lady, who knelt at the old oak tree?
And lo! the worker of these harms,
That holds the maiden in her arms,
Seems to slumber still and mild,
As a mother with her child.

A star hath set, a star hath risen,
O Geraldine! since arms of thine
Have been the lovely lady's prison.
O Geraldine! one hour was thine—
Thou'st had thy will! By tairn and rill,
The night-birds all that hour were still.
But now they are jubilant anew,
From cliff and tower, tu—whoo! tu—whoo!
Tu—whoo! tu—whoo! from wood and fell!

And see! the lady Christabel
Gathers herself from out her trance;
Her limbs relax, her countenance
Grows sad and soft; the smooth thin lids
Close o'er her eyes; and tears she sheds—
Large tears that leave the lashes bright!
And oft the while she seems to smile
As infants at a sudden light!

Yea, she doth smile, and she doth weep,
Like a youthful hermitess,
Beauteous in a wilderness,
Who, praying always, prays in sleep.
And, if she move unquietly,
Perchance, 'tis but the blood so free
Comes back and tingles in her feet.
No doubt, she hath a vision sweet.

What if her guardian spirit 'twere,
What if she knew her mother near?
But this she knows, in joys and woes,
That saints will aid if men will call:
For the blue sky bends over all!

PART II

Each matin bell, the Baron saith,
Knells us back to a world of death.
These words Sir Leoline first said,
When he rose and found his lady dead:
These words Sir Leoline will say
Many a morn to his dying day!

And hence the custom and law began
That still at dawn the sacristan,
Who duly pulls the heavy bell,
Five and forty beads must tell
Between each stroke—a warning knell,
Which not a soul can choose but hear
From Bratha Head to Wyndermere.

Saith Bracy the bard, So let it knell!
And let the drowsy sacristan
Still count as slowly as he can!
There is no lack of such, I ween,
As well fill up the space between.
In Langdale Pike and Witch's Lair,
And Dungeon-ghyll so foully rent,
With ropes of rock and bells of air
Three sinful sextons' ghosts are pent,
Who all give back, one after t'other,
The death-note to their living brother;
And oft too, by the knell offended,
Just as their one! two! three! is ended,

The devil mocks the doleful tale
With a merry peal from Borodale.

The air is still! through mist and cloud
That merry peal comes ringing loud;
And Geraldine shakes off her dread,
And rises lightly from the bed;
Puts on her silken vestments white,
And tricks her hair in lovely plight,
And nothing doubting of her spell
Awakens the lady Christabel.
"Sleep you, sweet lady Christabel?
I trust that you have rested well."

And Christabel awoke and spied
The same who lay down by her side—
O rather say, the same whom she
Raised up beneath the old oak tree!
Nay, fairer yet! and yet more fair!
For she belike hath drunken deep
Of all the blessedness of sleep!
And while she spake, her looks, her air
Such gentle thankfulness declare,
That (so it seemed) her girded vests
Grew tight beneath her heaving breasts.
"Sure I have sinn'd!" said Christabel,
"Now heaven be praised if all be well!"
And in low faltering tones, yet sweet,
Did she the lofty lady greet
With such perplexity of mind
As dreams too lively leave behind.

So quickly she rose, and quickly arrayed
Her maiden limbs, and having prayed
That He, who on the cross did groan,
Might wash away her sins unknown,

She forthwith led fair Geraldine
To meet her sire, Sir Leoline.

The lovely maid and the lady tall
Are pacing both into the hall,
And pacing on through page and groom,
Enter the Baron's presence-room.

The Baron rose, and while he prest
His gentle daughter to his breast,
With cheerful wonder in his eyes
The lady Geraldine espies,
And gave such welcome to the same,
As might beseem so bright a dame!

But when he heard the lady's tale,
And when she told her father's name,
Why waxed Sir Leoline so pale,
Murmuring o'er the name again,
Lord Roland de Vaux of Tryermaine?

Alas! they had been friends in youth;
But whispering tongues can poison truth;
And constancy lives in realms above;
And life is thorny; and youth is vain;
And to be wroth with one we love
Doth work like madness in the brain.
And thus it chanced, as I divine,
With Roland and Sir Leoline.
Each spake words of high disdain
And insult to his heart's best brother:
They parted—ne'er to meet again!
But never either found another
To free the hollow heart from paining—
They stood aloof, the scars remaining,
Like cliffs which had been rent asunder;

A dreary sea now flows between—
But neither heat, nor frost, nor thunder,
Shall wholly do away, I ween,
The marks of that which once hath been.

Sir Leoline, a moment's space,
Stood gazing on the damsel's face:
And the youthful Lord of Tryermaine
Came back upon his heart again.

O then the Baron forgot his age,
His noble heart swelled high with rage;
He swore by the wounds in Jesu's side.
He would proclaim it far and wide,
With trump and solemn heraldry,
That they, who thus had wronged the dame,
Were base as spotted infamy!
"And if they dare deny the same,
My herald shall appoint a week,
And let the recreant traitors seek
My tourney court—that there and then
I may dislodge their reptile souls
From the bodies and forms of men!"
He spake: his eye in lightning rolls!
For the lady was ruthlessly seized; and he kenned
In the beautiful lady the child of his friend!

And now the tears were on his face,
And fondly in his arms he took
Fair Geraldine, who met the embrace,
Prolonging it with joyous look.
Which when she viewed, a vision fell
Upon the soul of Christabel,
The vision of fear, the touch and pain!
She shrunk and shuddered, and saw again—
(Ah, woe is me! Was it for thee,
Thou gentle maid! such sights to see?)

Again she saw that bosom old,
Again she felt that bosom cold,
And drew in her breath with a hissing sound:
Whereat the Knight turned wildly round,
And nothing saw, but his own sweet maid
With eyes upraised, as one that prayed.
The touch, the sight, had passed away,
And in its stead that vision blest,
Which comforted her after-rest
While in the lady's arms she lay,
Had put a rapture in her breast,
And on her lips and o'er her eyes
Spread smiles like light!
                              With new surprise,
"What ails then my belovéd child?"
The Baron said—His daughter mild
Made answer, "All will yet be well!"
I ween, she had no power to tell
Aught else: so mighty was the spell.

Yet he, who saw this Geraldine,
Had deemed her sure a thing divine:
Such sorrow with such grace she blended,
As if she feared she had offended
Sweet Christabel, that gentle maid!
And with such lowly tones she prayed
She might be sent without delay
Home to her father's mansion.
                                        "Nay!
Nay, by my soul!" said Leoline.
"Ho! Bracy the bard, the charge be thine!
Go thou, with music sweet and loud,
And take two steeds with trappings proud,
And take the youth whom thou lov'st best
To bear thy harp, and learn thy song,
And clothe you both in solemn vest,

And over the mountains haste along,
Lest wandering folk, that are abroad,
Detain you on the valley road.

"And when he has crossed the Irthing flood,
My merry bard! he hastes, he hastes
Up Knorren Moor, through Halegarth Wood,
And reaches soon that castle good
Which stands and threatens Scotland's wastes.

"Bard Bracy! bard Bracy! your horses are fleet,
Ye must ride up the hall, your music so sweet,
More loud than your horses' echoing feet!
And loud and loud to Lord Roland call,
Thy daughter is safe in Langdale hall!
Thy beautiful daughter is safe and free—
Sir Leoline greets thee thus through me!
He bids thee come without delay
With all thy numerous array
And take thy lovely daughter home:
And he will meet thee on the way
With all his numerous array
White with their panting palfreys' foam:
And, by mine honor! I will say,
That I repent me of the day
When I spake words of fierce disdain
To Roland de Vaux of Tryermaine!—
—For since that evil hour hath flown,
Many a summer's sun hath shone;
Yet ne'er found I a friend again
Like Roland de Vaux of Tryermaine."

The lady fell, and clasped his knees,
Her face upraised, her eyes o'erflowing;
And Bracy replied, with faltering voice,
His gracious Hail on all bestowing!—

"Thy words, thou sire of Christabel,
Are sweeter than my harp can tell;
Yet might I gain a boon of thee,
This day my journey should not be,
So strange a dream hath come to me,
That I had vowed with music loud
To clear yon wood from thing unblest,
Warned by a vision in my rest!
For in my sleep I saw that dove,
That gentle bird, whom thou dost love,
And call'st by thy own daughter's name—
Sir Leoline! I saw the same
Fluttering, and uttering fearful moan,
Among the green herbs in the forest alone.
Which when I saw and when I heard,
I wonder'd what might ail the bird;
For nothing near it could I see,
Save the grass and green herbs underneath the old
    tree.

"And in my dream methought I went
To search out what might there be found;
And what the sweet bird's trouble meant,
That thus lay fluttering on the ground.
I went and peered, and could descry
No cause for her distressful cry;
But yet for her dear lady's sake
I stooped, methought, the dove to take,
When lo! I saw a bright green snake
Coiled around its wings and neck.
Green as the herbs on which it couched,
Close by the dove's its head it crouched;
And with the dove it heaves and stirs,
Swelling its neck as she swelled hers!
I woke; it was the midnight hour,
The clock was echoing in the tower;

But though my slumber was gone by,
This dream it would not pass away—
It seems to live upon my eye!
And thence I vowed this selfsame day
With music strong and saintly song
To wander through the forest bare,
Lest aught unholy loiter there."

Thus Bracy said: the Baron, the while,
Half-listening heard him with a smile;
Then turned to Lady Geraldine,
His eyes made up of wonder and love;
And said in courtly accents fine,
"Sweet maid, Lord Roland's beauteous dove,
With arms more strong than harp or song,
Thy sire and I will crush the snake!"
He kissed her forehead as he spake,
And Geraldine in maiden wise
Casting down her large bright eyes,
With blushing cheek and courtesy fine
She turned her from Sir Leoline;
Softly gathering up her train,
That o'er her right arm fell again;
And folded her arms across her chest,
And couched her head upon her breast,
And looked askance at Christabel——
Jesu, Maria, shield her well!

A snake's small eye blinks dull and shy;
And the lady's eyes they shrunk in her head,
Each shrunk up to a serpent's eye,
And with somewhat of malice, and more of dread,
At Christabel she looked askance!—
One moment—and the sight was fled!
But Christabel in dizzy trance
Stumbling on the unsteady ground

Shuddered aloud, with a hissing sound;
And Geraldine again turned round,
And like a thing, that sought relief,
Full of wonder and full of grief,
She rolled her large bright eyes divine
Wildly on Sir Leoline.

The maid, alas! her thoughts are gone,
She nothing sees—no sight but one!
The maid, devoid of guile and sin,
I know not how, in fearful wise,
So deeply had she drunken in
That look, those shrunken serpent eyes,
That all her features were resigned
To this sole image in her mind:
And passively did imitate
That look of dull and treacherous hate!
And thus she stood, in dizzy trance,
Still picturing that look askance
With forced unconscious sympathy
Full before her father's view—
As far as such a look could be
In eyes so innocent and blue!

And when the trance was o'er, the maid
Paused awhile, and inly prayed:
Then falling at the Baron's feet;
"By my mother's soul do I entreat
That thou this woman send away!"
She said: and more she could not say:
For what she knew she could not tell,
O'er-mastered by the mighty spell.

Why is thy cheek so wan and wild,
Sir Leoline? Thy only child
Lies at thy feet, thy joy, thy pride,

So fair, so innocent, so mild;
The same, for whom thy lady died!
O by the pangs of her dear mother
Think thou no evil of thy child!
For her, and thee, and for no other,
She prayed the moment ere she died:
Prayed that the babe for whom she died,
Might prove her dear lord's joy and pride!
    That prayer her deadly pangs beguiled,
        Sir Leoline!
    And wouldst thou wrong thy only child,
        Her child and thine?

Within the Baron's heart and brain
If thoughts, like these, had any share,
They only swelled his rage and pain,
And did but work confusion there.
His heart was cleft with pain and rage,
His cheeks they quivered, his eyes were wild,
Dishonored thus in his old age;
Dishonored by his only child,
And all his hospitality
To the wronged daughter of his friend
By more than woman's jealousy
Brought thus to a disgraceful end—
He rolled his eye with stern regard
Upon the gentle minstrel bard,
And said in tones abrupt, austere—
"Why, Bracy! dost thou loiter here?
I bade thee hence!" The bard obeyed;
And turning from his own sweet maid,
The agéd knight, Sir Leoline,
Led forth the lady Geraldine!

A little child, a limber elf,
Singing, dancing to itself,
A fairy thing with red round cheeks,
That always finds, and never seeks,
Makes such a vision to the sight
As fills a father's eyes with light;
And pleasures flow in so thick and fast
Upon his heart, that he at last
Must needs express his love's excess
With words of unmeant bitterness.
Perhaps 'tis pretty to force together
Thoughts so all unlike each other;
To mutter and mock a broken charm,
To dally with wrong that does no harm.
Perhaps 'tis tender too and pretty
At each wild word to feel within
A sweet recoil of love and pity.
And what, if in a world of sin
(O sorrow and shame should this be true!)
Such giddiness of heart and brain
Comes seldom save from rage and pain,
So talks as it's most used to do.

INDEX OF TITLES AND FIRST LINES

T 519855